Influencer Marketing

How to Build Your Successful Personal Brand and Passive Income Idea Through Social Networks Such as Instagram, Facebook, and YouTube for Beginners

JASON MILLER
&
RAY ROBBINS

Table of Contents

Introduction

Chapter 1:

    Pinterest --- 15

    Instagram -- 16

    Facebook --- 18

    YouTube -- 20

    Snapchat --- 21

    Twitter -- 21

    Others --- 22

    Why Social Media Marketing Works -------------------- 23

    How to Use Social Media to Generate Profits --------- 25

    Going Viral --- 28

    Formats Used in Social Media Marketing -------------- 28

    What Is an Influencer ------------------------------------- 29

    How to Find Influencers --------------------------------- 30

Chapter 2:

    Choosing a Name -- 32

    Logo Design -- 34

    Colors -- 37

    Consistency --- 38

    Convey a Message or Be Abstract? --------------------- 39

    Convey Your Ideal Customer ---------------------------- 39

    Always Brand Your Posts -------------------------------- 40

Making a Familiar Impression ---------------------------- 40

Bio --- 41

Choose a Branding Font ----------------------------------- 43

Voice and Tone -- 44

On Social Media – You Have Seconds ------------------ 44

How Serious Is Your Brand? ---------------------------- 46

Consider Multiple Accounts ---------------------------- 47

Take Stock of Where You Are -------------------------- 48

Actionable Steps --- 48

Chapter 3:

Plan Ahead -- 52

Be Clear and Concise ----------------------------------- 54

Message Focus -- 55

Active Voice --- 58

Focus on Benefits, Not Features ---------------------- 59

Think in Terms of Building Relationships ------------- 62

Give Away Valuable Information --------------------- 63

Social Media Is Interactive --------------------------- 64

"Which is better. Red or white? And why?" --------- 65

Start a Blog --- 65

Share News Related to Your Niche -------------------- 66

Post Infographics -------------------------------------- 67

Always Link --- 67

Call to Action --- 68

Mix Things Up -- 70

How to Stimulate Curiosity ----------------------------- 70

Special Requirements for Different Social Media Networks -- 71

Examples of a Good Post --------------------------------- 73

Chapter 4:

Setting a Posting Schedule -------------------------------- 78

Prep Time --- 80

Engagement --- 80

Don't Be Discouraged ------------------------------------- 81

Leveraging the Followers of Others -------------------- 81

Leverage Quora -- 83

Chapter 5:

Good Photographs --- 86

Simultaneous Posting ------------------------------------- 87

Posting Procedure --- 88

Helper Apps for Instagram ------------------------------ 89

Posting Frequency -- 90

Your Link --- 90

Instagram Business Accounts --------------------------- 92

First Step: Build Up Some Content -------------------- 93

Trading Posts -- 94

Paid Posting -- 96

Be Ready for Traffic ------------------------------------- 97

Summary --- 98

Chapter 6:

Setting up a Business on Facebook -------------------- 99

Creating a Facebook Page ------------------------------ 100

About Page -- 101

Facebook Page Button ---------------------------------- 101

Posting -- 102

Advertising -- 103

Chapter 7:

Posting Frequency --------------------------------------- 105

Video Length --- 105

Follow Examples --- 106

The Thumbnail Image ---------------------------------- 107

Setting Up Your Video --------------------------------- 111

Promoting Your Video on Other Sites ------------- 114

Earning Money from YouTube ------------------------ 115

Chapter 8:

Facebook Advertising ---------------------------------- 116

Audience Insights --------------------------------------- 117

Ad Type and Goal --------------------------------------- 119

Budget -- 120

Media -- 121

Platform Options -- 122

YouTube Advertising ----------------------------------- 123

Leveraging Videos -------------------------------------- 124

Budget -- 125

Chapter 9:

Work Now, Payoff Later ------------------------------- 126

Consistency Is the Key --------------------------------- 128

Free and Paid Traffic Leads to Passive Income ------ 129

Finding Offers to Sell ----------------------------------- 130

Affiliate Marketing -------------------------------------- 132

Chapter 10:

Email Marketing --- 140

Sales Funnel --- 141

Driving Traffic -- 144

Summary -- 147

Conclusion.. 148

Introduction

Congratulations on purchasing *Influencer Marketing,* and thank you for doing so.

The world has changed radically in the past decade. With the advent of social media and smart mobile phones, the media, communication, and marketing landscape was completely upended. It started early in the century with Myspace, which was quickly blown away by Facebook, which basically took their idea and did it much better. Meanwhile, YouTube was quickly becoming a popular website for watching videos, but it was dismissed as a silly pastime, where people went to watch funny "cat videos."

At first, Facebook almost operated under the radar. In the first few years, as it began growing in popularity, few realized the marketing power that the website had. Businesses were slow to notice and get on board. Everyone wondered how a website like that could make money. Nonetheless, the site kept attracting members and growing steadily.

At about the same time, the smartphone was invented, and Apple upended the world with the introduction of the iPhone, which was basically a handheld computer that had a phone in it. Again, at first, people didn't know what to make of it, and it seemed like an idle curiosity. About a year later, Apple then opened the app store. At first, people were putting a lot of games on the app store, and people didn't make the connection – what if you had social media on people's phones? At the time, a lot of hype surrounded the device, as individual software developers created rudimentary games that people could play on their phones, and many became instant millionaires.

This period introduced a whirlwind of change. Pretty soon, Twitter followed on Facebook, and other sharing sites like Pinterest continued growing. Perhaps observing Pinterest, some innovative entrepreneurs created Instagram, a simple app that allowed people to share photos with memes on them.

Fast forward to today, and you know the rest of the story. Now social media plays a prominent role in communication, marketing, and advertising. For business owners, social media has proven to be one of the most powerful tools available. Not only is social media powerful, but it levels the playing field.

If you are a small business or just an individual who is hustling online and looking to get customers, social media has opened up the world's markets to access in ways that have never before been possible.

In this book, we are going to help explain how small

businesses and individual entrepreneurs can exploit social media to grow their business and sell products. Reaching the public has never been easier, and different market segments can be targeted, often for free, and if not for free, at a low cost.

In this book, you will learn the most important social networks and what influencer marketing is and how that offers another channel that you can use in order to reach customers. And, as you will see, you can become a small "influencer" yourself, simply by putting out regular content.

After we come to understand Facebook, YouTube, Instagram, and other social media networks, we will investigate branding. You will learn simple and easy to implement tricks that can be used to brand yourself and create a presence on social media, which can turn into profits. We will explore the daily actions that you must take in order to build a following that will turn into actual profits.

As a part of your education, you will learn how to create effective social media posts. These posts can be put up as free posts, or used in paid advertising campaigns.

Then we will explore the idea of a sales funnel. Although the internet and social media has evolved rapidly, some of the same techniques still work. Among these is the concept of an email list and a sales funnel. One of the powerful ways that social media can be used with a small business is to push traffic to your sales funnel. If you have an effective sales funnel, it is not difficult to turn this traffic into profits.

YouTube is a great social media website; in fact, it may be one of the best. If you are able to use video to share content, it is relatively easy to build a large following and drive significant traffic from YouTube to your social media sites, and your sales funnel.

Finally, we will talk about paid advertising on Facebook, YouTube, and Instagram. Paid advertising is surprisingly low cost and powerful on social media websites. Simple advertisements on Facebook that cost only a few dollars a day to run can drive a lot of traffic. If you are going to pursue Facebook, advertising, you better be ready for the traffic! We will also talk about using YouTube and exploiting popular videos to get people's eyeballs on your products. YouTube advertising is similarly surprisingly inexpensive.

There are plenty of books on this subject on the market, thanks again for choosing this one! Every effort was made to ensure it is full of as much useful information as possible, please enjoy!

Chapter 1:

Important Social Networks

Welcome to the world of social media. In the past ten years, the communication landscape has been completely transformed. Although the old media is still around and frankly as big as ever, the attention of people is now split between many different communications technologies. And this is very good news for small businesses. The days of three network television stations and a couple of radio stations, which required a massive advertising budget to get any airtime, are long gone. In their place is a dynamic and easily accessible landscape where you can get followers and new customers without spending any money, and if you do spend money, you can use targeted advertising without breaking the bank.

The power to do targeted advertising is one of the most important reasons why your business should be on social media. You can zoom in on any demographic, location, or interest that is related to your business and your ideal customer. If you don't yet know your ideal customer, advertising on networks like Facebook is a great way to find out who they are.

The problem for many people in small business is they

don't really know which social networks they should be using to reach their prospective audience. Second, they aren't sure how to reach that audience, even if they have some idea which social networks are the most powerful. We hope to demystify these issues in this book. Let's get started by looking at the most important social networks that you should be using to focus your attention.

Important Social Networks

Social media has become incredibly diverse and fractionated. However, the major stalwarts remain where the action is. In our experience, Facebook, Instagram, and YouTube are King. In fact, these social media networks are so important that you could devote all of your time to using these networks, and you'd get all of the results that you want for your business.

That said, there are many social networks that can also be leveraged to bring in new customers. But which ones are really worth bothering with? The first thing is that it depends.

Knowing who your ideal customer is will be one of the central things that you need to keep in mind with your business. Of course, you already knew that because everyone in marketing knows how important that concept is. When you know who your ideal customer is, then you can target them more easily and effectively.

The first thing you want to think about is what gender are you marketing to. Is your customer base primarily female, male, or a fairly good mix of the two? How old is your typical customer? Are they 25, or 65? These are important things that need to be taken into consideration when using social media as a part of your marketing plan, because people of different ages, on average, can be found in different places. Let's take a look at the demographic data of some of the social media sites and apps.

Pinterest

If you read a lot of books on social media marketing, many of them are going to hype up Pinterest. And with good reason. According to the web traffic sit Similar Web, last month, Pinterest had an astounding 848 million visits. The bounce rate, which tells you how many people only look at one page and then leave, is about 43%, which is a pretty decent value. So, it sounds like you should be on Pinterest!

The reality is that it depends on what your business is about and who you are trying to reach. Let's start with gender. According to the Omnicore Agency, 70% of Pinterest users are female. The trend has become a little more balanced in recent years, with 40% of new signups actually being male users, but that still leaves men in the minority on the site. If you are marketing products that are of interest to men or to both genders, then Pinterest is not something you should be wasting your time on. On the other hand, if you are targeting young adult females, Pinterest might be exactly where you want to be.

Among active users, females are three times as likely to be an active user as compared to a male. And they trend young. Some 34% of Pinterest users are aged 18-29, and 28% are 30-49. Only 17% are 65+. So, if you are advertising hearing aids, trying to do it on Pinterest is probably not the ideal course of action. But if you are selling shoes for women made in hot colors – it might be exactly where you want to be.

Instagram

Interestingly, Instagram also trends female, although the demographics are far more balanced. Some 52% of users are female, so there is a slight imbalance. In the United States, it is estimated that 43% of adult females use Instagram, and about 31% of adult males use Instagram. Overall, 110 million Americans are on Instagram, and some 130 million users will tap on a shopping post to learn more about a product. A large fraction of American users, some 63%, look at

Instagram at least once a day.

If you aren't on Instagram with your business, you're already late to the party (but don't worry about it, it's never too late). It's estimated that 25 million U.S. businesses have an Instagram account. The app is extremely popular with so-called influencers, with surveys showing that nearly three-fourths of them list Instagram as their preferred social media site. The total possible reach on Instagram is 800 million people worldwide.

One of the factors that has made Instagram such a success is the fact that it's a mobile application rather than a website. Now you can reach Instagram through a website, but the overwhelming majority of users access it through the app. Why is this important? Because an app is something you always have with you since people are glued to their smartphones. An app also makes it easier to check, rather than jumping on a desktop computer to find out what is going on with some website. People still use desktop and laptop computers, of course, but an app just makes it easier for them to access. An app is also good for advertisers. Instagram is a simple visual medium where you can post images with a message or short 15 second videos. This opens up great marketing tools for small businesses.

Instagram opens up a little more of an older audience than Pinterest does, but 72% of teens are on Instagram, and only 31% of those aged 18-24 use it. Not sure why there is such a large drop-off, people who are aged 18-24 were young when Instagram came online about 8-9 years ago, you would think they would be completely accustomed to it.

In any case, the numbers are quite large – meaning it's worth utilizing for many businesses. Wouldn't you like to have instant access to 31% of 18-24-year-olds?

Facebook

Facebook is the granddaddy of social media sites. Although it has lost some popularity with teens and young adults, it remains a major workhorse. The great news for marketers is that Facebook has a very balanced audience, with more equal numbers among males and females, and a fairly even distribution among the different age groups. This may be in part because of the age of the site and its general focus. Facebook was around before smartphones, and the focus on linking family and friends is something that appeals to all age groups, including older folks. In fact, 62% of people aged 65+ who are online has a Facebook account.

The bottom line about Facebook is the audience is

enormous, and everyone is on there to one degree or another. Facebook has 2.4 billion monthly active users, making it one of the most trafficked websites of all time. Although 1.5 billion people access Facebook periodically using desktop computers, the platform also has a mobile app, and nearly everyone accesses it at least some of the time via the mobile app – including seniors.

Facebook makes it easy to target large audiences. You can do this using organic methods or paid methods or some combination thereof. Facebook not only lets people "connect" and share videos and images, it is also home to a large number of interest groups. People love to form online groups of like-minded people so they can discuss hobbies, sports, academic sites, or access support groups, and Facebook has made it very easy to do it. Rather than going through the hassle of starting your own website, you can leverage the Facebook website to create your own group, and millions upon millions of people do. You can also post messages to reach your customers, and the sharing capabilities of the site will help to automatically get your marketing exposed to larger numbers of people through people's various "friends."

As we will see later, advertising on Facebook is easy, quick, and cheap. You can also laser target advertising on Facebook in ways that have never been possible through the entire history of business.

In our view, no matter what you are marketing and who your target demographic is, you are going to want to be on Facebook.

YouTube

YouTube is nearly as big as Facebook, with some 2 billion monthly active users. It's estimated that some five billion videos are watched on the site every single day. About 73% of adults in the United States use YouTube, with about 60% of monthly active users being male. Nearly all U.S. adults use YouTube, and although there are more males than there are in the general population, it is easy to reach both genders on the site. It is also pretty well distributed among all of the age groups, and those aged 35-55 are the fastest-growing demo. YouTube is fast becoming the go-to source for how-to videos and tutorials, and it's also a place where you can find old music videos, news reports, and old tv shows, and funny cat videos are still quite popular.

The great thing about YouTube is that if you set up your videos the right way, you can get lots of organic views. And even if you can't get organic views, you can use advertising to reach people without spending hardly any money. YouTube is another site that is definitely a must when you are going for social media.

Snapchat

If you are looking to target younger people, the app Snapchat may be of interest. Snapchat is a messaging app that allows people to share images and videos. In recent years, it has become more popular for influencer marketing. However, the app is a little bit awkward, in our opinion, as compared to Facebook, Instagram, and YouTube. At this time, we don't recommend Snapchat for marketing purposes, but it is something to keep in mind as a possibility for the future.

Twitter

Well, everyone knows Twitter. Of course, it probably goes without saying that the site has drawn a lot of attention in part because President Trump uses it – either to great effect if you are a fan or as a menace if you can't stand him. Either way, you have to admit that he can draw a lot of attention using Twitter. Many celebrities are using Twitter to get their message out and to communicate with fans. It has its benefits, and it makes it easy for people to communicate and get short messages across. The site has become extremely political. Although the site is heavily trafficked, compared to some of its colleagues, it's actually on the smaller side. There are reported to be 330 million active users. The site tends heavily male, with some 66% of users being male. Only about 22% of US adults use Twitter, which is quite small compared to Facebook and YouTube. The number of users has declined, and in the 2016 election, and since it became highly politicized. The tweets that people put out have also become easy feeding for news outlets, who often build articles around what people are saying on Twitter.

So how is Twitter as an advertising and marketing platform? Our advice is to stay away from Twitter at the present time for advertising. Reaching people on Twitter with advertising is going to be a more difficult proposition as compared to say Facebook. It is easier for people to ignore ads on Twitter, and although the reach is certainly extensive, it's not very comparable to the heavyweights of social media. However, you can and should use Twitter as a regular user. Just stay focused on one topic and one topic alone. If you need to use it for several topics, create distinct accounts.

Others

There are many other sites that qualify as social media, including Tumblr, LinkedIn, TikTok, and Reddit. However, we just don't think they are worth it. They have smaller audiences, and there is not really anything to be gained by thinking of yet more apps and sites. Consider that if you concentrate on Facebook, Instagram, and YouTube, there isn't going to be a single connected adult that you are not going to reach. And, in our opinion, a business that puts some focus on its marketing efforts, rather than spreading itself thin trying to be at all places at once, is going to have a lot more success.

Why Social Media Marketing Works

There are three main reasons that social media marketing works. The first is the fact that everyone is on social media – of at least one type. Of course, we are exaggerating a little bit. There are probably some older folks who aren't using it, but as we saw above, even most people aged 65+ are on Facebook. The second reason to use social media, is the fact that it does a lot of the work for you. This happens because of the "sharing" capabilities that have been built into these platforms. Sharing allows information to travel around the world at virtually light speed. In the old days, to reach a large number of people, you would have had to spend a fortune to advertise on television, radio, or in national magazines. It would take a long time for your advertisements to go out, provided that you could actually afford it – and sharing would be by word of mouth only, if it happened at all. Someone might tell a friend that they saw a commercial for something interesting on TV, but the friend they told would not *see* the advertisement.

Today, things are completely different. A person who sees a post or advertisement you put up can share it with hundreds of their friends, instantly. This means that although you might pay for a certain number of views or clicks, you're going to get a lot of bonus clicks and views out of it that could increase the number of people who see your advertising by a large margin.

As an aside, we want to talk about magazine advertising a little bit. Of course, that is something that has moved almost completely online these days, but when we first started in the business, if you couldn't afford to get on television, you could use magazine advertising to reach a fair number of people. But what a difference that the world was. First of all, it was expensive. To get a full-page ad in a very modest magazine is something that would cost thousands of dollars. But even worse, it would take weeks to get the ad to run. You would place your order and then wait two months. Hard to believe, isn't it?

And what if the ad didn't work? Then you'd have to tweak it, and submit a new ad, and wait weeks for that ad to run, to see if it did any better. Compare that to Facebook, where you can have an ad reach an international audience within a couple of hours, and if it's not working, you can have a new ad in its place a few hours later. The differences are nearly beyond belief for those of us who were around running businesses in the 1990s.

Back to our discussion, the third major advantage of social media is that advertising on social media is cheap and targeted. In fact, although you could spend millions of advertising on social media if you wanted to, you can also advertise on it and reach a solid number of customers for just a few dollars a day. Social media is not only cheap, but it's easily scalable. And if you want to advertise to Females aged 18-24 living in Los Angeles or both genders aged 54-65 who loved Breaking Bad, you can do both. The targeting capabilities of social media advertising are unmatched.

How to Use Social Media to Generate Profits

The endgame of any business is profits. The key to social media is to use it to start building a relationship with your customer, which is one of the most powerful features that the platform has (maybe we should have mentioned it in the last section), and then leverage that relationship to push your followers into a sales funnel.

One of the biggest factors when it comes to online

marketing is trust. This is actually something that goes way back in time. More than a century ago, people were doing mail-order marketing. This was not any different than online marketing, other than the medium used to communicate differently. But consider this. In the late 19th and early 20th centuries, people would get marketing pitches, catalogs, and advertisements in the mail. Now, why would you suddenly cut a check to someone that sent you something in the mail? That idea sounds crazy when you write it down – and yet millions of people did and still do. But one of the factors that is important in that kind of marketing is that the marketer has to build trust and make it seem like you're their personal friend.

As marketing moved online soon after the Internet exploded in the late 1990s, the same principles held. One of the key jobs of an online marketer is to establish trust with prospects. That still holds true today, but one of the advantages of social media marketing is that the medium makes it very easy to build that trust you need in order to get customers willing to give you their money. With social media, you can talk directly to them, rather than just sending them a letter sight unseen. You can post videos of yourself, helping people to see you as a real person. You can take advantage of the two-way communication that social media provides to directly address any concerns people have.

The main goal, however, is to use social media to get fans, people are eager eyeballs who want to see your content. Some of the greatest internet marketers around will tell you that content is king – and that you should give away lots of content. Giving away content will improve your trust factor and also establish credibility. It will help to make you seem like an expert in a given area, and when you establish that, it's very easy to get people to buy from you.

The main thing to look for with social media, however, is the ability to use it as the front end of your traffic funnel. In the pre-social media days, Internet marketers relied on sales funnels and email lists to get people to buy their products. They offered a free product of some kind to do what we've been talking about, establish trust and credibility. In fact, in today's environment, sales funnels and email marketing are very much alive, but you can establish trust and credibility using social media before they even hit your website. This is like putting your trust and credibility on steroids. If someone knows and trusts you from YouTube videos and Facebook posts, when you ask them to visit your site and sign up for your free email newsletter, they are going to do it without hesitation. Social media can help you to dramatically increase your conversion rates at every step in your sales funnel.

Then once they get in the funnel, they are going to be far more ready to buy products, as compared to a lead that just comes across your website.

Going Viral

Of course, "going viral" is one of the great hopes of people on social media. When you create a great post that large numbers of people love, your post can go viral, which means (for the small number of people who don't know) that the post will be shared far and wide by large numbers of people. So, imagine a viewer of your post thinking that her friends definitely need to see this, and so she shares it with 20 people. Then each of those 20 people share it with 20 of their friends…and so on. This is something that wasn't even possible in the old days when people might come across a great advertisement on TV or radio. But today, it is possible to create a massive audience nearly instantly and get your products, ideas, and videos shared across the globe in a matter of minutes. For marketers, this is something that is truly revolutionary.

Formats Used in Social Media Marketing

When you plan on using social media marketing, plan on it being visual. You can always include texts with your posts, but you should focus on getting viewers thoroughly engaged. The fact remains that human beings are visual creatures, and so an image or a video is going to be far more powerful than posting words. In addition, you can always share hyperlinks – to your websites – on social media. This will help you get backlinks as well as getting people to visit your websites.

What Is an Influencer

An influencer is someone who has a large social media following. The following of an influencer is going to trust him or her, which makes the idea of being an influencer a very powerful concept in social media. Many of the fans of an influencer on social media are going to be checking daily to see what the influencer is posting. If the influencer recommends a product or a website, the fan base is going to take that recommendation seriously, and they will at least look at the linked product or website.

There are two reasons influencers are important. The first is that you can pay influencers – often small and reasonable fees – to either put up a post on your behalf, recommend your product, or recommend your website. There are influencers of many different sizes, and so you have a wide range of prices and options to work with. Some influencers may have 10,000 followers, and others might have 150,000 followers, while still others could have millions.

Another reason influencers are important is that you can become a social media influencer in your own right! Becoming an influencer is nothing more than getting a large number of followers. If you are posting daily, this will help you to keep your followers engaged and to keep adding more followers.

How to Find Influencers

The easiest way to find influencers is just to look at the number of followers they have. Alternatively, you can hire an agency to find influencers for you that will post on your behalf for a fee. Some influencers that have relatively large followings but numbers that are not huge might be willing to do trades with you, which can help you get followers of your own without spending money.

Unfortunately, Instagram has made the strange decision to not allow likes to be displayed in the United States any longer. This action may backfire on them, but at the time of writing, it's too early to tell how it's going to work out. This may make it harder to find out who would really benefit you in the influencer game.

This brings us back to Twitter because although we don't generally recommend Twitter, we do recommend it for using influencer marketers. Many celebrities, large and small, have rabid followers on Twitter. And one easy way to drive traffic is to have an influencer on Twitter recommend your product or website. So, don't use Twitter for advertising or to devote a large fraction of your day tweeting, but do consider using it if you can find influencers to pitch your product or website, provided that the audience of the influencer is going to be relevant to your business.

Chapter 2:

Brand Building on Social Media

Building a brand for your business is going to be important for success on social media. It helps bring recognition and recall. In some cases, you can be the brand. This is something many people who train internet marketers do. There are many steps to branding yourself, and we will discuss those and how to integrate them on social media. The most important thing is to be consistent so that you can build recognition across multiple platforms.

Choosing a Name

A name to use for branding is an important first step. If you are an unknown, the brand name should include a short phrase that describes your industry. Internet marketers like Frank Kern can get away with branding his own name because he has been well known for 20 years. But that doesn't necessarily mean you can't brand yourself, but it takes time. Branding yourself will involve repeated postings on multiple social media outlets, and it will probably require a lot of YouTube videos, so that people can see you discussing your niche – which will help to establish yourself as an expert in your niche. Expertise in your niche is what helps with branding.

Alternatively, you can associate with your product. Looking on ClickBank, there are several products aimed and Forex traders. Forex is the foreign exchange where currency is traded. One product is called "Forex Trendy," and they have several customized graphics. If you were promoting Forex Trendy, you could incorporate the name of the product and some of their graphics (which they provide for affiliates) into a brand name. The word Forex is something that is already widely searched, and so that is something that will give you a major leg up in getting found by users.

That is one problem with using just your name as a brand, at a time when you are not well known. Of course, there are ways around this, but going back to the Frank Kern example, his name is something many people are searching for on Google and other sites because he is renowned for giving marketing advice. John Doe, however, isn't as well known if he is known at all – so it will take a long time to get the name John Doe (insert your name here) known as an expert in his niche. But if you incorporate some keywords, then you can leverage the keywords to help build expertise.

So, when you choose a name that you are going to brand, decide if you are going to make yourself the expert that people seek out, or if you are going to make the product something to seek out. As a middle ground, you might hope to brand a company name. This is possible as well, but this faces the same issues as using a personal name in the early stages of your growth. When you create your company name, say it's Acme Services Inc., in the early stages, nobody knows the company name or associates it with your niche. So, a part of your work is going to be associating the name with an important keyword related to your niche, so people begin to build that idea in their head that Acme Services provides expertise on Forex trading, or sells makeup, or whatever business you happen to be in.

Logo Design

Unless you are artistically inclined, we don't recommend designing your own logo. But we definitely recommend having a logo. All companies have a logo; it's another way to get yourself implanted in people's minds and to help them to remember and recognize you. Remember that human beings are visual creatures, and a logo will help implant your brand into their minds. Another way that a logo can help you is that when you are leveraging social media, whether it's YouTube, Instagram, or Facebook, you are going to be posting a lot of images and videos, and including a logo on your media is going to help establish your brand. Also remember that if you are making quality images and videos, people are going to be sharing them with their friends. If you have a professional-looking logo that is on your media, that means every time that you get a share, a new person is going to see your logo, and that helps to expand and establish your brand.

Like we said, unless you are artistically inclined and truly good at graphics design, you shouldn't design your own logo. We also don't recommend using a canned logo from a stock photo site. That might save you money, but if you are serious about building a business, saving money is not something you should have at the top of the list. Think in the long term when it comes to your business. Your logo is going to stay with you for a long time, so you might as well get it done right.

The good news is you don't have to break the bank to get a unique, professionally designed logo. One website we constantly utilize for professionals that can do small tasks for us is Fiverr. If you haven't heard of Fiverr, it's a website you can use to hire independent contractors to do small jobs for you. The original idea was that the job would cost $5, but prices have gone way up as the years have gone by. However, you can find many excellent logo designers that will make a unique and professional looking logo for around $70-100.

INFLUENCER MARKETING

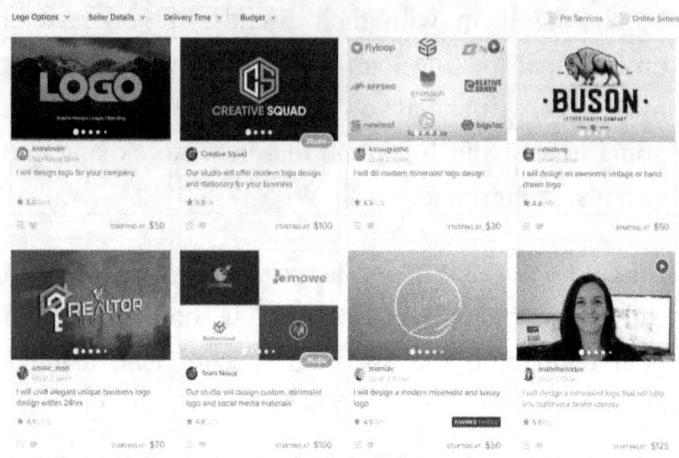

There are a few requirements that you should have for your logo:

- The designer should provide the full-size image that they come up with so that you have it at full resolution. Then you can make copies of it at various sizes that you will need.

- Make sure it has a transparent background. You want to be able to place it on images and on screenshots used on sites like YouTube, where you can create video thumbnails for displays in searches.

- Don't accept mediocrity. Remember, this is something that is going to stay with you and your business for a long time, possibly years, so make sure it gets done right.

- Carefully evaluate past examples that the designer has made. If they don't show many, ask them to send samples. Tell them they can watermark the samples to make it more likely they will share them.

- Read reviews. Fiverr has orders of past reviews, and you will be able to find out if the designer has had past issues with late deliveries or low-quality work.

Colors

Having colors that go together is an important aspect of a logo or any other graphic. There are many guidelines on choosing the right colors that go together. You can just let your designer go with whatever they like, or you can come up with colors on your own and discuss it with them. A good way to get colors that belong together is to use color wheels. There are many websites that have information about choosing colors that blend well; here is an example.

https://brightside.me/article/the-ultimate-color-combinations-cheat-sheet-92405/

A solid, single color is good for branding when it comes to social media. Choose a color that is going to stand out. It can be combined with white, using a color for an image and white for the name of the business.

But remember that you are going to be using your logo on images, which means a single-colored logo isn't always going to work. You might need to have an alternative logo for use on images with a dark background, for example. An easy way to get around this is to have the designer made a colored logo, and then have them make a version of the logo that is solid white for darker images.

Consistency

In order to successfully brand yourself, your business, or your product, it is important to have consistency across all of your platforms. Imagine if Coca-Cola used a different brand name or logo for network television, cable, and YouTube. You would mistakenly think that there were different companies selling soft drinks. The same principle works for you, so you need to settle on a good design and then stick with it. Use the same name and logo on Facebook, Instagram, Twitter, Pinterest, or any social media platform that you choose to engage with. A unified presence is going to help you build your brand much faster and get the recognition that you need.

Convey a Message or Be Abstract?

When designing a logo, an abstract design is fine, and you are just trying to create a visual image that sticks in people's minds to get them to remember you. However, if you can also convey some kind of message, that can help you increase the value of your logo. The message can be a simple one, and you might want some kind of icon in the logo that will represent the industry that you are in. Or it might be something a little more abstract. If you are a business consultant, you might want to show someone "thinking" to convey the idea that you are going to help your clients with ideas. This is not a critical step, many designers are good at creating abstract images that are memorable, and that is what you are really after with the graphic that is in your logo.

Convey Your Ideal Customer

Knowing who your ideal customer isn't just important for deciding which social media platforms to use and where to advertise, it is also going to be important for your logo designs. Of course, you can go with an abstract design that is simple and has appeal across demographic groups, but if you are specifically targeting one demographic group, that might be important for the design of the logo as well. So, if you are targeting females aged 18-30 or male video game players, you might want completely different logos. Be sure to communicate to the designer who your ideal customer is if you feel that it's important. For some businesses, you might be targeting multiple demographic groups on different platforms, and so you might want variations of your logo by color.

Always Brand Your Posts

To build a brand, always branding your posts is going to be an important step. If you are inconsistent when it comes to branding, then it's not going to be effective. So, you are just going to have to make it a part of your routine to use the name you have settled on and to always include your logo on your posts. The logo doesn't have to be front and center (although it can be at times), you can put it off to the side in a corner. But make sure it's visible as long as it's not interfering with the image. You can also use your logo when creating Facebook pages and so forth to help people identify you and solidify that brand.

Making a Familiar Impression

The point of the logo is to get something that people are going to start seeing all over the place and something that they will associate with and remember. Think about famous logos that you might immediately recall, like Nike, McDonalds, or Amazon. Just seeing the Nike logo by itself will be something that is recognizable. You aren't going to have their reach, but you want that logo and your brand to begin to be implanted in a smaller scale audience, to help breed familiarity. Remember what we discussed in the last chapter; trust is an all-important concept when it comes to online marketing. Branding is one way that you can start to build trust and familiarity. Familiarity by itself is something that is going to increase the trust of your prospects.

Bio

When you sign up for social media platforms, they are going to have a small space where you can enter a bio. Take some time to write a good bio that quickly conveys who you are and what you can do for people. For the purposes of branding, you want to have one bio that you use across all social media platforms. Like the logo, the bio is going to be important for stamping in people's minds some familiarity and is an opportunity to make a connection to the niche of your business. If you have a bio that is different on different social media platforms, this is going to be confusing, and it will work against creating consistent recognition.

One part of your bio is going to be a cover image. In the example below, we show the image used by the company Burt's Bees. Notice that the image has a hashtag that they have associated with their brand. The hashtag conveys a message that they want to incorporate as their company's mission. You should sit down and think about something that is similar. It doesn't have to be a hashtag, but that can be a helpful way to get your brand shared on many social media platforms. But if you don't want to use a hashtag, you can just add a short phrase to your image. If you use a plain image, it might look nice, but by adding the short hashtag, they have turned the image into something that is uniquely theirs while we recommend hiring a professional to get our logo designed when using images for cover photos and so forth using a stock image site is fine.

Notice also that Burt's Bees has consistency. The images below show their home page on Twitter and Facebook, and they have the same logo and the same cover photo, and the hashtag is mentioned in both places. The subtle use of colors is good as well, as subtle seems to work better than loud.

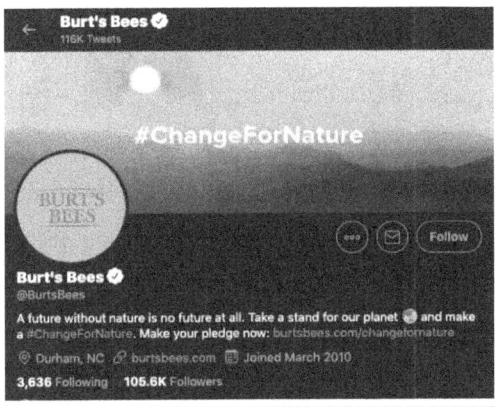

Choose a Branding Font

You might not think about this too much, but any text used in your branding should be consistent as well. Experiment with different fonts in a word processing or image program to see what you like best. You can use Photoshop or a free to download image program like Gimp to play around with making text to use on your cover photo and see which fonts you like best – and which fonts seem to be connected to your brand or product.

Voice and Tone

When you are writing text to help brand yourself, think about the voice that you are going to use in your marketing. This is going to be something that is going to depend on who your customers are. You aren't going to use the same voice with a customer base that is 50+, as you would with a customer base that is 18-24. But no matter what voice you are using, one thing that remains true across all demographics is you want to be sincere and genuine. Try and communicate how you personally relate to your customers. Hopefully, you are promoting a product or service that you would find valuable yourself so that you can put yourself in your customers' shoes and speak to them directly. Try to avoid obscure messages. In your bio, for example, a short sentence that clearly and quickly conveys what your business is about is going to be important.

In a way, showing you the Burt's Bees profile might have been a mistake. Don't misunderstand – it does everything right. But Burt's Bees has been around for a long time, and was already well established before social media platforms were big. So, they can afford to be a little vague.

On Social Media – You Have Seconds

When people are on social media, especially when it

comes to mobile apps, their attention span is very short. They are anxious to click or swipe to the next thing, and so you might only hold their attention for a couple of seconds. It's important to set up your logos, cover photos, and your bio to immediately convey what you are offering. While a big, well-known brand like Burt's Bees can afford to wax on about the value of nature without saying what their product is (everyone who is visiting their site already knows what it is, and has probably seen their products in person), they have no idea who you are. So, you have that two seconds to tell them who you are and what you are offering them in the first sentence of your bio. Some social media platforms may be pretty restrictive in the amount of text you can include in your bio, so make sure that your text:

- Is completely clear and worded simply.

- Tells them what you can do for them in the first sentence.

- Speaks in a plain tone that is friendly – don't try telling a joke or use sarcasm.

- Don't try to be profound. When you are beginning the branding process, the point is to communicate clear information about what you can do for your customer, not that you are going to save the planet.

To get some ideas, look up some brands on Instagram, Twitter, or Facebook to see how they have set up their bios – but look for small to mid-range brands. In other words, avoid looking at well-established global powerhouses like Burt's Bees that are not looking to convey who they are (because everyone already knows). Look for smaller companies that are not so well-known to get ideas.

How Serious Is Your Brand?

Some brands need to convey a serious tone. Using emojis in your images or brand logo doesn't help convey seriousness. Are you selling stock market tips? Then you probably don't want to come across as glib or humorous. Interestingly, if you are selling fashion, perfumes, makeup, and the like, you don't want to come across as humorous either. If you are in a niche where there are many big players, study some of the advertising that they are using. Consider that Estee Lauder is not going to be having some guy in the basement, putting up their Instagram posts; they are going to hire professional ad agencies to do it. So, you can learn from what the big brands are doing and mimic it when appropriate. Try and focus on big brands that are the most relevant to your niche.

Consider Multiple Accounts

You aren't restricted to one Instagram account or Facebook page when you are a business. If you have a varied customer base, consider creating multiple accounts on the same social media platforms in order to communicate with each demographic directly. This can be an important part of your branding since you can include sub-niche targeting. If you are selling a product that appeals to 65% females and 35% males, you certainly don't want to leave potential male customers on the table, but the way you communicate with your main customers might not appeal to the males in your audience. So, you can have a sub-branding effort that you could utilize on different social media platforms. You can even use different logos for this purpose if you want to, but keep in mind that you don't want to spread yourself thin when you are trying to launch your business on social media. Consistency in posting on a regular basis and responding to comments by users is going to be an important part of running your presence online. So, make sure that you have the time to spend effectively managing multiple social media accounts before you decide to pursue that path. If you create a sub-branding account but only post to it once every two weeks, then it's not going to add much value to your overall efforts.

Take Stock of Where You Are

Once you settle on your branding, you will need to keep track of your activity and the responsiveness of users to see if it is effective. Testing in the early stages is always good. With that concept in mind, you might not want to settle on a single logo in the beginning. If you are on a budget, it's understandable that you will only have one logo and a branding name. But if you can afford it, you might do some experimentation. See if using different logos changes the level of engagement. Don't be afraid to change logos and brand names early on, if the indications are strong that it's not working. In most cases, however, the branding is going to be secondary to the quality of your posting.

You can even survey people to see what they think is better. Consider setting up an online quiz and paying a mid-level influencer to send traffic to the quiz, where you can show the audience alternative logos for them to vote on.

Actionable Steps

Now that you understand what branding is within the context of social media, it is time to get started with branding your business.

- Start by looking at your audience, or who you

think your audience is going to be if you haven't built anything up yet. Determine whether or not you are going to need to split up your social media marketing efforts for different demographics so that you can get a clear picture of whether or not you might need different social media accounts, logos, and cover photos to target different demos.

- Do some research on color palettes to get an idea of the colors you would like to use in combination with your branding. Color is not an all or none issue, remember that you can have the same logo in a variety of colors.

- Think about what wording you want to include on your logo. It should at least include a signature with the name of your company.

- Jump on Fiverr and hire a designer to make your logos.

- When the designer is working on your logo, write a short bio. Make sure the first sentence tells the prospect exactly what you do. After you've made it clear what you offer customers, then you can tell them who you are. Remember that different social media platforms are going to offer different amounts of space for information like bios. But also remember that no matter what, attention spans online are short. So, it's important to be clear and convey as much information as possible in the first line.

- Create a cover photo that will be used across social media platforms. The cover photo can be, but doesn't have to be directly related to your business. Add a short phrase to the cover photo that will help with your branding, as we discussed above. If you are not good at making attractive looking images with text on them – hire your graphic designer for a second job and let them make the cover photo for you. Remember that this is really important, so you want something that looks really good.

- Create your accounts once you have all the images that you need to get started. If you are looking to get feedback on different logos, either run them across friends and family or try and do a survey. If you can't find an influencer to hire, you can run a short ad campaign on Facebook to get a few hundred people to vote on the best logo.

- Keep consistency across your accounts. This is the case even if you have multiple accounts to target different demos. Within each demo, but consistent.

- Maintain a tone of voice for your demo. Remember that you are going to speak differently to people that are different ages, genders, and possibly race or ethnic groups or countries. If your brand is global, you might even have a different social media account for the US and Canada, and Australia or Japan, for example.

Chapter 3:

Elements of a Good Post

Social media platforms are going to vary in the details, but there are some common elements across platforms and some general principles about posting that you should follow. Something that we noted with branding is that it's essential to be consistent. While posting on Twitter or posting on Facebook or Instagram will have their differences, maintaining a consistent persona and brand across all the different social media platforms is something that is going to be important. In this chapter, we are going to discuss some of the elements of a good post that we think you should adopt to get the most out of your social media marketing efforts.

Plan Ahead

Posting on social media is easy. For regular people, that's usually fine. But for a business that is actually a problem. The last thing that you want to do is to post impulsively. When you are using social media in order to promote a business, we advise carefully planning each of your posts. That doesn't mean you have to spend an entire week planning it out, but you should sit down and spend a few minutes to half an hour planning out each post. You can duplicate the post for all the social media platforms, customizing it as necessary but conveying the same message.

First, sit down and decide the reason behind the post. If there is not a reason to post, then you shouldn't post. Of course, you want to be posting frequently, and we do advise posting on a daily basis or at least a few times a week. The fact is, the more you post (to a point), the more rapidly you are going to gain followers. However, posting frivolously is far worse than posting at all.

The important thing to consider here is that you should focus on looking at the post from the perspective of your customer. Your post should have a purpose, and that is to convey the benefit of your product or service to the customer. Alternatively, another valid reason to post is to share information that is of value to your niche, even if you aren't personally providing it. So perhaps you are selling makeup products with your business. Maybe you're having trouble conveying something about your business on a given day, but that doesn't mean you can't post. Find an article with tips that would be relevant for your niche that isn't recommending a specific product, and then share it with a comment on your thoughts about the article. This is a great way to build rapport with your audience, because it conveys the sense that you are sharing a common interest with them, and that you aren't just about selling things. By sharing valuable information without asking anything in return, you can really help to build up trust.

So, planning begins with the reason for your post. When you sit down to plan, write down the purpose of your post in one sentence. Then decide whether you are going to post an image or a video. What message are you going to convey in the media that you present? Start with a clear and concise message. Remember that on Instagram or Pinterest, users are just going to focus on the short text message that is on the image. Keep that in mind as you think about it.

If you are going to make a video, whether it's a long video for YouTube or a 15-second "story" for Instagram, you also need to think about what you are going to convey in the video. We will talk more about this in a bit.

Be Clear and Concise

Whether it's a meme on an image or text that accompanies your social media posts, conveying a simple and clear message is one of the most important aspects of a social media post when you are trying to promote a brand, product, or business. It is better to make your messages clear and to the point, rather than trying to be super clever and mysterious. Remember that big brands have a lot more room when it comes to these types of decisions. We can go back to Burt's Bees social media profile – remember that they are already very well known by their prospects. Even people who haven't used their products have seen their products in many brick and mortar stores. Such a brand like that can afford to focus on flighty and high-minded messages. You can't afford to do that when building a completely brand-new brand. Even if you have a local business that is successful, it's not going to be known across the country or in different countries, so you have to use every interaction as an opportunity to educate the public and let them know what you offer them, and on a secondary level who you are and why they should trust you.

Message Focus

There are a few principles that you can think about when designing your posts that will help you to immediately connect with users. Think about the main point that you want to get across with your post, and then think about 2-3 secondary points that you are hoping to convey. Put these in the outline form.

The first principle is to be specific in what you are trying to say. A fluffy and feel-good message that might make a given Instagram post popular for just sharing around and giving people warm and fuzzy feelings is not going to help you sell products. Don't use any vague language in your posts. Be specific in what you are trying to say so that the reader will have a reason to click through and buy from you at some point. That doesn't mean you should be hard selling in your posts, and you should be working to build credibility and value in your niche.

A second aspect of your message focus should be long-term consistency. Don't give followers the feeling that sometimes someone else is posting, or give them a completely different feel from one post to the next. This is one reason why it is good to have multiple social media accounts if you are going to be targeting different demographics. Try and maintain a solid level of consistency at all times.

Concise is better than long-winded when it comes to social media. Remember the basic facts that we have stated multiple times already – you have just a second or two to grab people's attention. Being concise makes it more likely that you'll be able to pull them in.

Being concise doesn't just mean writing a short sentence, but short sentences are better when posting on social media. It also means using shorter words. Long and complicated words, especially words that people have to pull up a dictionary in order to find out what you are talking about, are not the kinds of words that you want to use in social media, either directly in images or in accompanying text. If you have trouble thinking up short words to use in your posts, jump on thesaurus.com, and look for equivalent words that can convey the same meaning with fewer letters.

Abbreviations and acronyms are also to be avoided. Even some of the most popular abbreviations are not going to be known by everyone, but all of your users are going to speak basic English. Unless you can't completely avoid it, try and avoid using abbreviations in your posts. Only use an acronym if it is very widely known and specific to your niche. For example, if you are selling something to airline pilots, it would be fine to use the FAA.

You might think that if you are marketing to young people, using acronyms and in vogue phrases is acceptable. In a way, it is, but remember that your social media leaves a long-term trail. Five years from now, unless you delete it, your post is still going to be there. Acronyms and phrases used by 18-year-olds today are going to be largely forgotten in a few years. For that reason, it is better to speak in plain English. Young people are still going to get a concise and plainly spoken message that is in plain English, and the benefit of this is that it will solidify your presence on social media over the long term. If you use some catchy phrase that isn't going to be in use a few years from now, your post might become worthless. Remember that as new teenagers get older and get in your demographic, you still want to sell to them, and they might be using totally different lingo than the generation that came just before them. But (hopefully) they will still be speaking English.

Active Voice

Marketers always advise writing in active voice, in preference to what is known as passive voice. When you are using an active voice, you will describe the subject in a sentence as taking action. This can be a little bit confusing to new copywriters, but if you are using an active voice, the subject in the sentence acts on the verb in the sentence. In passive voice, the subject is acted upon. Past-tense words like "was" can be a signal that you are writing in a passive voice. The distinction can be a bit subtle, however, so let's look at a couple of examples.

This is an active voice:

Women love shoes.

Jamie is playing Candy Crush.

John logged into his Facebook account.

The passive voice version of these sentences:

Shoes are loved by most women.

Candy crush was played by Jamie.

Facebook was used by John.

So, remember that passive voice conveys the past to some extent. The subject of the sentence in the passive voice is secondary or coming at the end of the sentence. Active voice is preferred in marketing because it is focused on a definite assertion or action by the subject. Passive voice is a weaker way to state the same message.

Focus on Benefits, Not Features

One of the oldest lessons when it comes to writing marketing copy is to focus on benefits rather than features. Of course, you are going to state your features, but that is a secondary aspect of your marketing efforts. Although you might not think of posting on social media as writing sales copy, you are basically writing a sales copy to promote your business, product, or service on social media. So, start thinking in terms of benefits. New marketers may not be familiar with the distinction between features and benefits, but it's actually an easy concept to understand.

- Benefit: A benefit is the result that the

customer gets from using your product or service.

- Feature: A feature is a specific characteristic of your product or service.

Think about a nice umbrella. The features of the umbrella might be the color or the material the handle is made out of . The benefits are being shielded from the hot sun or a rainstorm. "Stay dry even during the worst of times" would be a benefit, "Red color with a mahogany handle" are features. You might want to convey both, but the phrase about keeping out of the rain would be what you place on your image, and if you have a text description that accompanies the image, you can put some of the features in there.

Sometimes it is going to be difficult to think in terms of benefits, but think of someone using the product or service and what it will actually do for them. If you can convey the benefits of using your product or service, this is really going to help drive followers and sharing on social media platforms.

One of the differences between stating features and benefits is that benefits tap into people's emotions, while features tap into people's logic. Emotions are more powerful and fundamental. Again, you are going to want to convey both benefits and features to a customer, but you are going to hook them with benefits, not with features. Features are extra icing on the cake. But in the end, they are going to make a decision to buy largely based on emotion most of the time, and by emphasizing benefits, you can help to ensure that they are going to buy.

Another way to understand the benefit vs. feature dichotomy is that with benefits, you are showing the customer your product or service, even if you are just painting a picture in their minds. With features, you are telling them about it. Showing someone your product is more powerful than telling them about it. And a part of showing someone your product is to get them imagining themselves getting the benefit from it.

An example of a feature would be for a car manufacturer to state that their vehicle got 40 miles a gallon. The benefit would be the money saved from having to buy less gasoline.

When you think of benefits, put yourself in the shoes of your prospect. Think about how your product or service is going to make their life easier, more productive, or help them in some personal way, and then state that to them in your social media messages.

It is important to avoid sounding mechanical in your

messaging. One of the best ways to convey benefits is to tell a story about it, and social media platforms are often the perfect way to do it. Think about what a buyer would want to accomplish with your product or service and then show someone getting that benefit in a short video or even a still image. The video stories for Instagram are perfect for this, but remember they are short duration and so conveying the benefit in a short amount of time can be challenging. The flip side of this is that conveying benefits quickly is really going to help your marketing efforts. Imagine that you were selling electric cars. A quick way to show the benefit would be to film yourself, driving the electric car down a country road, or maybe even past a gas station where people are waiting in line to fill up. Then you could use a tagline like "Never have to fill up again."

Think in Terms of Building Relationships

Not every post that you put up should be prodding people to buy something. The primary reason that you are using social media platforms is to build a relationship with your prospects. This is a slow and long-term process, but it will pay off by helping you build a loyal following of customers that will not only buy your products down the road, but they will share your information and recommend your products or services to their friends and associates.

Remember that people don't like the hard sell. The old joke used to be the worst person to be around was the used car salesman, and that is what helped give rise to CarMax, a business that is built around the idea that you are not going to be pressured by a high-pressure salesman. So, avoid doing the hard sell all the time, especially in the beginning. Your first priority should be establishing yourself as a friendly niche expert.

Think about bonding when you are putting up your social media posts. We have to assume that you are going to pick a niche for your business that you know about, which means also knowing the inside language and views of the audience in that niche. If you aren't sure about it, spend some time studying the niche, including following others that are already promoting on the niche to see what kind of insider language and thoughts they are passing back and forth.

Give Away Valuable Information

Any marketing expert is going to tell you that one of the best ways to succeed with marketing is to give away valuable content. This creates value, and it will help you bond with your followers if you show that you are willing to show them expertise and share valuable information without asking anything in return. If you are selling a physical product, you can write articles about using products like it or related products in the same niche. If you are selling an information product, you should share valuable parts of that product for free. For example, if you are selling a video course, if the course has 20 videos, don't hesitate to put snippets of the videos with valuable information up for free. You can even share an entire video. If your content is good, that is one of the best ways to whet people's appetites and get them ready to spend money on the entire course. Think of it as test driving a car. Someone is more likely to buy after test driving a car than they are without test driving the car. Of course, not everyone will be interested and end up buying, but that is beside the point.

Social Media Is Interactive

Remember that social media is a two-way street. This is not like advertising on television or radio where you just throw something out there and then forget about it. Social media is a two-way street, and people are going to be commenting on your posts. You are not necessarily going to have time to interact with all your comments, but you should make it a habit to respond to one or two comments in every post. That makes you open, accessible, and engageable.

In fact, you should go beyond this and actively request

conversation with your followers. One way you can do this is to ask a question at the end of the post, and invite readers to respond. For example, say you were selling wine glasses. You could post a picture showing a bottle of red wine and a bottle of white. Then ask:

"Which is better. Red or white? And why?"

Everyone will have their different opinions on this, of course, but the point is it's an open-ended question that is going to get people involved. That will help solidify your brand presence and have people thinking about you – and also thinking about coming back to visit. And notice that we never once mentioned selling wine glasses, rather we avoided selling altogether but focused on something that would of interest to the same people that would be your customers. Asking interesting questions that people might have strong opinions about will also help to get your posts shared.

Start a Blog

Yes, it's a whole new level of extra work – but having a blog can be a great way to leverage your social media. When you have a blog, you don't have to put a huge amount of effort into it, because we are not talking about creating a blog for the sake of becoming a blogger. Instead, we are going to use our blog in order to have a place where we can put longer and more detailed posts to provide interesting and relevant free content for potential followers. Let's say that you have an idea for seven tips for wearing makeup. You can write this up in a blog post, and then make an image with something like "7 tips for looking your absolute best" on a picture of a woman putting on makeup. Then you link back to your blog. This will help engage readers and get them to follow you since they will be encouraged that you are providing free and valuable content. But remember that if you take this approach, this is not going to be something that you want to do only once or just now, and then, you should do it at least twice a week. Get into the habit of writing a blog post say every Tuesday and Friday and then posting links back to the blog post from the various social media platforms that you are using.

Share News Related to Your Niche

As a part of your effort to convey that you are an expert in your niche, take some time to regularly share news related to the niche. Let your followers know that you are actively engaged with the niche and actively following the latest news related to it. If you go about this the right way, by posting timely and relevant information, for many people, you can become the go-to source for information related to that niche, and this will lead to more followers and later on more people who are buying what you're selling. You will also get more shares if you are posting relevant information on the latest news in the niche.

At times you can just post news and information, but at other times, find ways to integrate the latest news about your niche with the products or services that you are selling. If you can connect your brand with some breaking news about the niche, this can be a powerful way to draw in buyers. But don't force it. Only make a connection if it is natural, and it comes across as honest and sincere.

Post Infographics

An infographic is an image that also includes useful blurbs of text. Of course, make sure that the text included in the image is relevant and useful.

Always Link

No matter what social media platform you are using, always link back to your website. The best place to link back to is a signup form for your sales funnel. Use abbreviated links created by a URL shortener. Include the link with every post and in your bio. Don't throw it in people's faces, but have it there to make a connection available when your posts arouse curiosity. If you are posting something that is a hard sell, then you can say something with the link like "Signup here" or "Click here to buy." If you do not include links back to your main website, you are missing opportunities. When posting on YouTube or Facebook, which allows a lot of text content with your post, you can post multiple links in the same message. In that case, you can include a direct call to action for the link, and you can also post a link to your blog. You should also post links to all of your social media accounts. So, on YouTube, at the end of your video description, put links to your Facebook and Instagram accounts. Also, link back to your blog. Think of this as a signature that you put on every post. Likewise, share a link to your YouTube Channel and Blog on Facebook posts.

Call to Action

A call to action is just a request that the audience does something. In some cases, you are going to directly ask them to purchase your product. This is perfectly fine as long as you are only doing it periodically. If you ask people to purchase something every time that you post, that is going to make you look salesy, and that is going to turn people off. But you need to do it at times. Otherwise, you might not drive any visitors that actually buy.

But there are other types of call to action that you can use on social media. You can use people who see your post to help drive it to a larger audience. Again, you don't want to be a pest here either, but you can ask for help in sharing your message now and then. Ask them to share it with friends and family, and one thing you can do is come up with a hashtag for a post that you can use to get people to share and re-engage.

Later, we will be talking about sales funnels and email lists, and as a part of your business, you are going to want to have a signup from where people can join your email list. An email list is valuable because it's another way to directly join up with and communicate with a group of people that are interested in what you are selling. The email list itself is going to be a more warmed up audience. That is, they are going to be people that are actually interested in buying something. You are going to use social media to drive traffic to the email list, so one call to action should be periodically using is inviting people to sign up to join the list. When you are on social media, you aren't going to necessarily state that you are asking them to join the list to sell to them, you want to tell prospects that you have a free newsletter and that you are going to give them some free information that is going to be valuable to them if they sign up. Remember to keep your promise so that you will maintain credibility.

Mix Things Up

Don't post the same way every single time. First and foremost, mix up your media. That means you should post short videos at times, and post images at others. If you only post single images, it can help, but your profiles are going to be more effective if you post different types of media. You can leverage one social media platform on others. For example, you can post a video to YouTube, and then you can post the YouTube video on Facebook and Twitter. So, you don't have to make a new video specifically for the other platforms. This will also help to get followers from Facebook or Twitter to also follow you on YouTube.

How to Stimulate Curiosity

An effective technique to use in posting is to ask a question. This can either be in a post title or on an image. The question should be designed to get the viewer curious and interested. Going back to the electric car example, even though this isn't really practical it illustrates the point, you could use a question such as "What would it be like never having to buy gas again?"

Use a question to get the wheels turning in people's minds, and do it in a way that is going to make them interested in following you and purchasing your products.

Special Requirements for Different Social Media Networks

Posts on different social media platforms are not all going to be the same, even though you are going to be able to share some commonalities in many cases. If you are posting a single image, that is something you can do on virtually all the platforms. However, there are going to be a few differences.

- On Facebook, you can also include a lot of text. Doing so may or may not be appropriate for a specific post. If you decide to post a lot of text on Facebook, think about ways to make the post relevant to people who are going to read the entire post and also for people that are only going to skim it. One way to do this is to break up the post into sections, with each section making a point that can be summarized with a short, concise sentence. Write down what that summarizing sentence is, and then use it as a bold sub-headline that you can head off the section with. That way, someone who is going to be skimming the post can simply read the headlines to get the gist of it, but those who want the gory details are able to do so also.

Facebook actually doesn't have special requirements, and it actually gives you a lot more possibility. You can even post text-only content on Facebook, but remember that while you can do that now and then, you probably don't want to make that the focus, because you want to draw people in with visual imagery and video.

- Of course, YouTube is video only, but you can use images that you are posting on Instagram with your YouTube video or make meme images specifically for YouTube. We will talk more about this later, but YouTube allows you to upload custom thumbnails. This is the image that is going to be displayed when your video shows up in a user search. The purpose of the thumbnail is to attract attention and draw the user in so that they take the time to open your video. In many cases, Instagram images are not going to be appropriate to use on YouTube because a good thumbnail is going to be one that someone can look at and read what the video is about.

- Twitter has a character limit. It was recently expanded from 140 characters, and we believe it is now 210 characters at the present time. That is still a short bit of space, and so if you are going to use Twitter, you will need to convey your message in concise language. But remember that you can post images and videos on Twitter as well. Although users on Twitter are more accustomed to reading text, they are still going to be drawn in by images and videos. Twitter is also a good place to use for simply sharing news items related to your niche, but with your commentary attached. Be sure to use hashtags on Twitter.

- On Instagram, the focus is going to be images and video stories. Short and to the point, with hashtags to help with searches. When you are thinking of posting here, don't bother thinking in terms of text. Your focus should be on the text message that is placed on the image.

- Pinterest is going to be quite similar to Instagram. Focus on the image.

Examples of a Good Post

In this section, we'll look at some examples of good posts that can inspire you. In the first image, we have a bank of America "pin" that was posted on Pinterest.

INFLUENCER MARKETING

Let's take a look at some of the reasons this is a good post. The first thing is the name of the business, and the logo is prominently displayed at the top of the image, but they are not intrusive. Second, there is a woman in the photograph who is a customer. Why is that important? Remember that we noted most users of Pinterest are female.

Presumably, this is going to help viewers *see the*mselves using Bank of America. The message conveyed in the text is that you are growing your business. When you are analyzing the post, you know that what they are selling is a business loan, but they never state that. Instead, they have listed a benefit – Grow Your Business. A feature would have been "get a loan now with 2% interest". See how much more power you have when stating a benefit? Also note that the woman looks very happy – happy that she is growing her business, and presumably making more money.

Finally, besides the woman in the picture, the most prominent feature of the post is the large text : TAKE RISKS. For entrepreneurs, this is going to speak directly to them. Entrepreneurs see themselves as risk-takers, and they know that in order to build a successful business, some degree of risk-taking – maybe it's just trying to get by without a 9-to-5 job – is a fundamental part of the lifestyle. This is an excellent post because it hits the demographic, it communicates simply and clearly, and it speaks to the niche directly. It also conveys what they are selling but without even stating it.

When you are posting on say Facebook, you are going to want to have a catchy headline to go with the image. So, you might state a benefit in the headline.

Chapter 4:

Daily Actions and Overall Approach

Now you have some idea of what a good post involves. This is something that you should study in detail. Log into the social media platforms that you are interested in and look for posts that have a large number of likes or posts by people with a large number of followers. Then take time to study the different elements that are in the post and how they help with marketing or building a brand. Again, shy away from posts by celebrities or "influencers" that have millions of followers. What they are going might work simply because of their already existing fan base and name recognition. Look for other businesses that are in your niche, or mid-sized influencers to see what they are doing that is engaging followers.

Once you know what to post, the next thing to focus on is how to post. To build a following on social media, you are going to want to get a regular schedule setup. The key to success beyond simply posting good content is to post good content on a regular basis. The more you stick to a schedule, the fast you are going to grow a significant following that will turn into buyers of your product and service. While you can get instant viewers using paid advertising, we recommend building up a little bit of content before you start driving paid traffic. You want people to come to your profile and see that there is something here, rather than just checking out a single post that is unlikely to make them follow you. Also, try and get some family and friends to follow you when you launch your profiles. Social proof is one of the most important concepts in marketing, and if someone sees that you have some followers and likes, it will help to encourage them to give you a follow as well. The sad truth is that nobody wants to be the very first person to follow you even though this is all online. So even if you can only get a handful of friends to follow you and like the first few posts that you put up, it will help to convey the perception that you are engaging, and others are liking your content. This will make new visitors feel more comfortable and willing to do the same. You can also use paid advertising to drive likes, and we will discuss that in a later chapter.

Remember that posting for the sake of posting is not something that you want to get in the habit of doing. So, if you are tired or stressed and can't think of anything useful to say, it is better to just leave posting to another time or even another day. Posting worthless content is not going to help your followers stay engaged or get them to share your content with their friends.

Setting a Posting Schedule

We recommend that you take daily actions on your social media accounts. If you are able to do so, posting 2-3 times per day on Instagram is even better, but it's not essential. You don't want to post too much, and you should only post with a frequency that is compatible with the value that you can offer. Once a day is a good schedule for most people, and one of the ways to make it more feasible is to limit yourself to no more than four social media platforms, and as much as possible, use the same content across different platforms. Remember that if you create a video for YouTube, you can post it to Facebook and Twitter, and if you create an image for Instagram, you can post it to Pinterest, Facebook, and Twitter. So, there is going to be a lot of overlap that is possible between the different social media platforms, and while the overlap may not exact, this means that you can usually design one post and share it on multiple platforms, rather than having to plan out a post for a single platform and do that for each one.

YouTube is one exception to our general rules. The first thing to think about with YouTube is that even if you are only posting short videos with a few minutes of talking, it is going to take more time to plan and execute. The longer your videos, the more prep time you are going to need in order to get them up. With YouTube, a once a week schedule might be sufficient. Remember that you want to provide a lot of value when you are posting YouTube. You aren't going to want to just post of video saying, "Hey, John is here. I'm just hanging out." So, it's acceptable to prepare and wait a few days before posting. Also, remember that your ability to share YouTube videos on some social media platforms may be limited or not available at all. But because of the large audience on YouTube, if you are able to create original video content, it is definitely a must.

Keep in mind that you don't have to start off with a set rule. For social media posting to be effective, it must be frequent and regular. There is a lower limit beyond which you are going to be slowing your impact to the point where it's not worth doing. In our opinion, posting once or twice a week is far too infrequent. It will take a very long time to get a following that way, and posting infrequently is not going to keep your following engaged. At least three times a week is a minimum for posting to Facebook, Twitter, and Instagram. It is better to post daily on those platforms. On Twitter, posting a few times a day, as long as it's relevant, is even better. Of course, posting on Twitter can be easy, and you can leverage your other posts, so take an image from Instagram and post it on Twitter too. Again, YouTube is the exception, and less frequent posting is acceptable.

Prep Time

Begin your day with a 20-30-minute time frame that is used for prep. State the goal of your post and come up with a concise and engaging statement that can be used as a headline. Then decide which platforms to post on. Since it is fair use to put anything you develop for other social media platforms on Facebook, we recommend thinking of Instagram or YouTube first, and then posting the content used for that on Facebook and Twitter. You can then elaborate if you feel it is helpful since you can post extra text on both platforms.

Also, have a standard signature that you use, which will have backlinks to your sales page or email landing page, your blog, and your other social media sites.

Engagement

Check up on your accounts 2-3 times per day in order to engage with followers. It is important to keep engaged with them and respond to comments and questions in a timely manner. Each time that you put up a post, be the first person to comment. This can help drive conversation and let users know that you are a real person who is willing to talk to them in the comment section. You don't have to make social media your life, but if you put some effort into engagement, the more productive your efforts on social media are going to be. Generally, we recommend posting one comment yourself and then reacting to 2-3 comments that other people post.

Don't Be Discouraged

In the beginning, you are not going to get much attention on social media. It takes time to build up a good following and have an active user base. So, you might feel like you are all alone in the world in the early part of your social media marketing career, but don't get discouraged. Over time, you will build up a following as long as you are putting up relevant and valuable posts. Persistence is going to be the key to success over the long run, and those who are able to push through the early stages, which are not going to seem like they are productive are going to be the ones who succeed in the end.

Leveraging the Followers of Others

There are many things that you can do in order to increase your followers across networks that don't involve spending money. The first thing is to put a link to one of your posts – when it's relevant. In other words, go on the feeds of other people in your niche and when there are posts that you can contribute to, leave a meaningful comment and leave a link back to one of your posts. The important thing in regards to this approach is that you avoid being spammy, and you use the technique sparingly. You don't want to come across as someone who is desperate to drive traffic back to their own posts, so only do it when it is directly relevant.

One way to make sure that you can do it when it's directly relevant is to look at other people's feeds for content that you can post about, too, with your own unique spin on it. When you find something, then put up a post on your own feed, and then return to the original post and figure out a way to relate it back to what you posted.

A good way to do this that seems less intrusive is to link across platforms. So, let's say that you put up a YouTube video on a given topic in your niche. Then you can jump on Facebook and Twitter and look for people that are discussing the topic, and then make a comment, and suggest that they check out your YouTube video. You can also use this method outside traditional social media, posting in blogs and forums. The only thing to keep in mind about blogs and forums is many of them have rules about trying to sell things, especially affiliate marketing products; in other words, that is prohibited. But if you have content that is purely informational in character, such as a helpful YouTube video, it should be OK to post it in most places.

Leverage Quora

An interesting website to leverage in an effort to get followers is Quora. If you are not familiar with it, this is a question and answer website. People post questions on Quora about virtually any topic, and you can answer questions and include links back to your posts. The only thing about Quora is they don't like spamming, and so you should take the time to only post there if you can provide a detailed and thoughtful answer to questions about your niche that people are posting. One thing you should never do on Quora is posting a direct link to an affiliate marketing product or a sales page, even if it's your own sales page. But what you can do is post links to relevant social media posts where you can add more value. For example, if your expertise was plumbing, you could post a video on YouTube where you show how to fix a leaky bathroom faucet. Then find questions about this on Quora, and post a verbal explanation about the process in response to the question, with a link back to your YouTube video.

Avoid spamming even if you have something relevant to say. So, don't open up Quora and post a link to your video in response to ten different questions over the course of an hour. Just post it once and then find some other reason to answer a question. The backlinks will help to drive your content, and people seeing it on Quora may be interested in checking out your video.

Chapter 5:

Instagram

In this chapter, we are going to specifically address the topic of using Instagram as one of your primary social media platforms. This is a great platform to use, but there are some caveats. The main thing to consider when using Instagram is that the audience is going to tend younger. That doesn't mean that it is exclusively a younger audience, but if you are marketing something that is relevant to senior citizens, this is not where you want to be spending your efforts. If you have something targeted at young adults, this is definitely the place where you want to be. If you are marketing something that is sufficiently general that any adult is going to have potential interest, then Instagram can be a part of your overall social media marketing strategy.

Another factor to consider when using Instagram is to ask yourself if the product or service that you are offering is suitable for the platform that Instagram offers. Although they have recently allowed posting of video, the videos that you can post on Instagram, so-called "stories," are only 15 seconds long. Second, despite adding video content, it remains primarily an image sharing site.

Of course, that still leaves the door open as a marketing platform. In the old days, advertising in magazines was a powerful way to pull in customers. Many advertisements in magazines are full-page photo ads. So, in a way, magazine ads were the Instagram of their day. Although it might not be immediately obvious, start thinking about ways that you can promote your product or service using a photograph and brief message and drive traffic back to your website.

Good Photographs

The first thing that is required for marketing on Instagram is a good photograph. This might put you off. Do you need to have a photograph that you personally take? The answer is no. So, it would be a good idea to sign up on a stock photo site where you can get a large number of downloads per month so that you will have access to some professional photographs that can be used at least in part with your Instagram campaigns. If the photograph looks good, the message conveyed with it is going to be more important than whether or not the photograph is yours or one from a stock image site.

We advise study before taking action, so that you can get the most out of your efforts. So, take some time to learn your way around Instagram. First of all, create an account. It is possible to have linked accounts with Facebook since they own the app.

Then browse around to find images that are related to your niche. Study the images that look the best to find the elements of a good Instagram posting. Of course, we never advise directly copying someone, but a bit of mimicry, especially when you are first getting started, is not going to hurt. The basic rule is finding out what is already working and do exactly what they are doing.

There are two ways that you can post. You can post a plain image, or you can post an image with an overlaid text. As a marketer, you are probably going to want to include some text along with your logo (but don't make the logo prominent). You can create the image with text as you go, or you can make it ahead of time.

You can also add some text to your posting. This is not going to be an extensive amount of text, so you need to learn to get straight and to the point when you write text to accompany your posts.

Simultaneous Posting

One of the nice things about the Instagram app is that you can use it for simultaneous posting to Facebook, and you can also share on Twitter. So, if you have a good image that is ready to go, this will help you save time.

Posting Procedure

The procedure for posting on Instagram is quite simple.

- Prepare your image ahead of time. As a marketer, you aren't going to want to post impulsively and should have everything planned out. Think about the benefit you want to convey, how that benefit is going to be expressed in the image and what text you want to use to convey your message, and the text caption to include with the photo.

- Instagram allows hashtags to help with search when people are looking for topics related to your image. Write down a list of 8-12 hashtags to use before you go ahead with the post (we want to avoid thinking on the fly, so that is why we advise doing it now).

- Open the Instagram app and click the + button. Select the image from your camera roll (be sure to save it to your camera roll before beginning this process).

- If desired, you can run the image through one

of their filters.

- The final step is to add your caption and hashtags. You can also opt for Facebook posting here as well, and other options like setting the location.

We advise that you make your profile more interesting by mixing up media. You are going to have to put either a video or an image when you post to Instagram, so you are not going to be able to post text only. However, you can post abstract images with text on them, or even create a solid black or white background and put text and a logo on it. In any case, you should post videos on Instagram periodically in order to make it more interesting.

Helper Apps for Instagram

There are many apps that can help you prepare your Instagram posts. Some of them will help you add text if you want to or make other adjustments that you find necessary. They can allow you to post directly to the app or save to your photo library, and then you can open Instagram to post directly.

You can also find apps that help you create video stories for Instagram. Helper applications for this purpose are also available online for a price. It can be worth making a small investment for these tools, since they can help you make your videos look professional, and they will be perfectly formatted for posting to Instagram.

Posting Frequency

In order to build a following, we recommend that you post 2-3 times per day. Posting on Instagram is something that is going to take a little more effort because a little more frequency of posting is best for this site. The good news is that posting on Instagram is pretty easy, so it's not going to be too time-consuming overall.

Your Link

One of the most important things with Instagram is your profile. The profile allows you to enter a short bio – and most importantly, you can put a link there back to your website. We recommend that you build an email landing page that is directly related to the sales of your product, and that you use this link as your website link on your Instagram profile. This will help to drive traffic to your main website as you start to build up a significant Instagram following.

Second, be sure to add a good profile picture. However, we advise using your logo as your profile picture. Remember, this is about branding and promoting your business, not you personally. There is one exception to this, if you are going to be building a business brand around yourself as some kind of niche expert or coach, it may be appropriate to use your own image as a profile picture.

It is also allowed to include an email address, so you can include an email address that you want to use for business purposes here. Just be sure to answer relevant inquiries that you might receive (and take that as an opportunity to send people a link to your email landing page). This is an example of an Instagram profile. Notice that their link is found just below the bio (right above the Follow, Message, and Email Buttons):

When we click the link, it does what we just advised – it opens up a signup form:

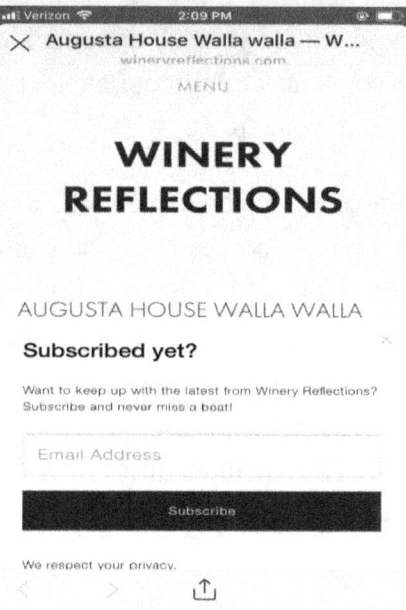

That isn't necessarily the best landing page in our opinion -but the function is perfect, and this illustrates how you should set up your Instagram profile.

Instagram Business Accounts

If possible, we recommend keeping the personal and the business aspects of your life separate. There might even be legal reasons to do this, but there are many practical reasons as well. Instagram allows you to create business accounts, and this can include niche-specific Instagram accounts. You should utilize this to help you drive your business. At the time of writing you can create up to three niche accounts with a business, and so this can be a way for you to post to Instagram targeting specific niche market segments, or if you are offering different products and services that are not directly related, you can use the different accounts to promote each individual niche.

First Step: Build Up Some Content

Yes, this process is going to take some patience, but it will pay off for those that follow it. In the following sections, we are going to talk about some ways that you can leverage other Instagram accounts to help drive traffic, but before you do that, you want to establish your own presence on the platform.

So, this is going to involve posting frequently with good content for a period of time. Again, we recommend that you post 2-3 times per day on average. Before you approach anyone else or use paid advertising, our advice is to follow this procedure for a month. That way, when you go and approach another Instagram account, you will look substantial as, by that time, you will have somewhere between 60-100 posts. You want to look like you have something of interest that will benefit the followers of other Instagram accounts so that you can offer to make trades. People who see that you only have 2-3 posts are not going to be interested in dealing with you.

We also recommend a warm-up time to build up the number of your posts even when using paid advertising. That way, when people go to your account as a result of your paid advertising, they are going to see that you have substantial and interesting content already, and they are likely to give you a follow and perhaps like and share some of your posts. Again, aim for some variety. Video doesn't have to be a major component of your posting, but after the first month, you should aim to have about 3-4 video stories on your profile as well. If your profile has some content and it's more interesting, people are going to be more likely to visit the link on your profile and even sign up on your email list.

Trading Posts

After you have gone through phase one of your Instagram life, the time is right to start making an effort to drive traffic. The first trick to use in order to gain some traffic and more followers is to seek out small and mid-sized Instagram accounts that have between 10,000 and 50,000 followers. Then you are going to ask them to promote your account in exchange for you promoting theirs.

Every Instagram account has a direct message button

and email address on the profile page. Try direct mail on Instagram first to contact them. If they don't respond, send an email (some accounts might not read their Instagram messages). If they don't respond after sending the email, don't pester them and move on to another account instead.

Since you have a new account, you are going to have to offer them a little more than what they are giving you. A typical arrangement is that an influencer account will offer you a post on their account for a certain amount of time, or they will recommend to their own followers that they follow your account, again for a certain amount of time.

One approach you can take is to ask them to put up a post for say 12 hours or a day, and in exchange, you will put up a post directing people to their Instagram account for 3-5 days. That doesn't sound fair, but in truth, it is fair if they have 10,000 followers, and you only have 100.

Before taking this approach, you might want to run some paid advertising so that you can get some more followers on your own, and make the offer a little more attractive.

You can make this offer to several different Instagram accounts. Don't do more than one at a time, but try to do one a week. See what the results are, if you are able to build up a lot of followers and you can keep finding people that are willing to post and recommend a follow, this procedure can keep working for you.

Paid Posting

One of the interesting things about Instagram is that you can basically do paid promotion without any involvement of Instagram at all. The way to do this is to approach an account with a larger following, direct message them and ask them if they accept paid postings. Of course, everyone likes to make a buck, and many influencers on Instagram make their money this way. So, it shouldn't be too hard to find Instagram accounts that are willing to promote your account for a price.

The amount of money required is going to depend on the size of the account. You don't have to go for the gold and try getting paid promotions with the largest accounts, but expect to pay more for someone that has a million followers versus someone that has 50,000 followers.

When you contact them, ask them what their fees are in order to make this kind of arrangement. In addition to a flat fee for posting on your behalf or recommending that their users follow you, they may have a scaling price depending on the amount of time the post is left up. For smaller accounts that might have 50,000 up to 250,000 followers, they might charge you anywhere from $35-$200 to leave your post up for 12 hours or 24 hours. People set their own rates, so we can't give you exact amounts that are going to be charged for large Instagram accounts in your niche, so you are going to have to start contacting people in order to find out what it's going to end up costing.

You can also try contacting people to directly promote your product or service, if you are confident in it. They might want to get a free sample, or you can shoot them a video demonstrating the product. If you make games or apps, Instagram influencers can be a great way to get some direct traffic, if they recommend the app on their profile.

Be Ready for Traffic

Later in the book, we are going to talk about landing pages and having an email marketing list. Before you do anything, you should have that setup. The point is that you have to be ready to leverage any traffic that might come your way and capture leads. Otherwise, you are wasting your time. When a large Instagram account is driving traffic to you, people are going to be checking out your profile, and some of them are likely to click on your website link. So that is something you are going to have to set up before you use Instagram for promotional purposes. While the main reason that you are going to be paying people for exposure is to get followers to build a long-term relationship with on the social media platform, and so you aren't necessarily expecting immediate signups or sales, you should be ready in case some people are willing to sign up or even buy your products.

Summary

Instagram is a great app, and the nicest thing about it is, provided you can get or take engaging photographs and write great captions or put great text on your images is that it's easy to use. Posting frequently on Instagram is not something that generally takes a huge amount of effort, and the platform makes it easy to link back to your site. The second advantage of Instagram is the ability to directly contact influencers that already have large followings and get them to promote you or even your products.

Chapter 6:

Facebook

Facebook remains one of the most powerful social media marketing tools that are available. Even if it is not your primary platform for promotion, it can be leveraged to get more reach, and one of the most powerful tools that we are going to consider in chapter 8, Facebook advertising, is the best reason to have a presence on the site. You can also use Facebook advertising to run the same ad on Instagram. That is actually a good way to test to see if your products are relevant for the Instagram audience without putting in the effort to build an Instagram profile. You can run ads on the platform through Facebook and see what kind of response they get. If you find that you aren't getting many clicks or reactions, then that would be telling you that Instagram is not an ideal social media platform for your product or service.

Setting up a Business on Facebook

You must have a personal profile on Facebook, but you should search Facebook for business and set up a business account on top of it. It is a fairly easy and straightforward thing to do. This is going to be something you'll want to do for the purposes of advertising. Even if you are not going to advertise on Facebook right away, you are going to want to have this step-in place.

Creating a Facebook Page

For a direct presence on Facebook, creating a Facebook page for your business is going to be the way that you promote your business on Facebook. A Facebook page is associated with your personal Facebook account; however, the association is not direct or public. People will only know about it if you invite them to the page. Whether you invite friends or family to the page is going to be entirely up to you. But for those that are concerned about privacy and keeping the business postings on Facebook separate and distinct from your personal profile, it will do exactly that for you.

The first step is to jump on Facebook and select pages. It will then allow you to visit Facebook pages that you have created, or you will be able to make a new page. When you create a new page, the first thing that you will do is to create a name for your page.

As we stated earlier, our advice is to have a uniform presence across platforms for your business. And so that means if you have created an Instagram page for Acme Wineries, you should name your Facebook page

Acme Wineries as well. Also, use the same logo and cover photo across your platforms.

Facebook is going to ask you for your profile photo to put on the Facebook page. Here, you want to use your business logo. Then it will ask you to add a cover photo.

About Page

Next, you will probably want to go to your About page. The About page allows you to enter general information about your business, including phone number, address, and so on. You can also add a mission statement and fill out "Our Story," which is basically a spot where you put a bio for the business. Facebook is a lot more extensive than other social media platforms, so you can be far more descriptive with text when filling out this information. The Our Story section can have a cover photo, headline, and text. If relevant, you can also add team members to this section.

Facebook Page Button

On the main Facebook page, you are going to notice that just below the cover photo, there is a section that says, "Add Button." Don't ignore it! This is a chance to put a call to action button to take visitors to your

Facebook page to your website. You can use it to direct users to a shop or to sign up for your email newsletter.

Posting

After you have everything set up, you can start posting. Our recommended frequency for posting on a Facebook page is 3-5 times per week up to daily. Keep our admonition in mind, however. If you don't have something worthwhile to say on Facebook, just let it go until something comes to mind. Facebook is more content-intensive, and so you should be sure to add value to your postings.

Think of posting on a Facebook page as a Facebook account for the business. We discussed posting earlier, and you should follow the advice in that chapter, but the basic idea here is that you are going to be posting on the business page in the way that you would post on your own Facebook profile. But the key is to keep things relevant and informative. Don't post anything frivolous on a business page.

One of the reasons for having a Facebook page is to tie things together. So, when you post a YouTube video, post it on your Facebook page as well. When you post a photogram on Instagram, also post it on your Facebook page. If desired, you can do that directly from Instagram, but we actually recommend using the same image but posting directly to the page and adding some more text content.

From time to time, you can also use it as a place to post simple text. The point is to make it useful and engaging for any visitors that come across the page. The longer your feed is, the more time they are going to spend on the page, and the more likely they are to follow you and share your posts.

Tying together a blog – assuming you have one – is also something that you want to use Facebook for. Each time that you post to your blog, grab the link to the post and then post that on your Facebook feed.

Advertising

We are going to be talking about advertising on Facebook in chapter 8. So, we aren't going to go into the details here. But the main way that we prefer to use Facebook is for paid advertising. In our view, the Facebook page is secondary, and we will use it to help give some extra exposure to our other sides and social media accounts.

Chapter 7:

YouTube

Making videos isn't a requirement, but we highly recommend it. Video is one of the most engaging ways to interact with people using social media, and YouTube is one of the most massively trafficked websites on the planet. If you get good at making videos, you can use it to demonstrate expertise in your niche or to demonstrate products that you are selling. You can integrate it with any kind of business. If you have a Shopify store, you can use videos on YouTube to showcase your products, and then link directly back to the product on the store. You can also use YouTube to demonstrate expertise in a subject area if you are selling information products or affiliate products. They also let you post affiliate links with your videos, unlike some other sites.

The good news is that you only have to be decent at making videos, you don't have to be the best person, have the best voice, or be the most photogenic. The approach that works the best with YouTube videos is to be natural and relaxed. Another good thing about it is you don't have to worry about not being so good at first. Remember that everyone starts somewhere. Second, you will get better with time, provided that you make videos on a regular basis.

Posting Frequency

YouTube production is a little more involved than posting on other sites, and so it's not necessary to be posting daily. In fact, that might even harm you if you are not able to put the time in to make a quality video on a daily basis. If you can post good videos daily, and some people will find that it comes more naturally to them, that is fine. But if you can't, don't worry about it. Our recommendation to build a following on YouTube is to post between 1-3 times per week.

The amount of production involved in making your video is going to, in part, determine how frequently you can post. Some people simply set up a webcam or use their mobile phone and talk to the camera. If you can do that effectively and your videos are not very long, you'll be able to post more often.

Video Length

The most important thing in a video is engaging content that provides useful information. A video doesn't have to be an hour long. It can be as short as 3-5 minutes, if people get something useful out of it. Of course, the shorter videos are more likely to be viewed all the way through the end, but remember that you are using YouTube as a tool, and not necessarily as an end in itself. So, you want your content to be significant enough so that people are going to check the links that you place in the video description and visit your main website.

There are not any firm rules, but unless you have something really compelling to discuss or you are offering some sort of video course or coaching, and you want to post samples, you don't want your videos any longer than 15-30 minutes or so. The short attention span of online users is a factor on YouTube, as well. It may be the case that the information you have to offer is so useful, and your presentation is engaging enough to keep people on your video that long, but people are always anxious to move on to the next thing when they are online. In many cases, a five to seven-minute video is going to be appropriate.

Follow Examples

Before you start making videos, look at what other people in your niche are doing. This is another example of finding the expert and do exactly what they are doing with your own spin on it. So, research your niche on YouTube, first to see if people are getting significant numbers of views to make sure that there is an audience for you on the site. More than likely, there will be because quite frankly, everyone is on YouTube at least some of the time.

The second thing you want to look for is what kind of content are they offering, and how are they offering it. You will want to make videos that are a similar format if they are getting a large number of views. You can also make videos on similar topics. Of course, once again, you don't want to copy anyone, but you should certainly use inspiration and use what already works.

Something that we strongly advise is that you get a free plugin for your web browser that is called vidIQ. This handy plugin will help you spy on the competition. One of the things that it does is it pulls out the keywords that are used as tags by a given video. If you are able to see what keywords videos in your niche are using to drive a lot of traffic, then you will know to use some or all of these keywords on your videos as well.

Also, look at the title and description of popular videos. Pay special attention to how they set up their title, as this is one of the most important parts of the video.

The Thumbnail Image

The thumbnail image is often an afterthought when people upload YouTube videos. Of course, that isn't the case for experience YouTubers that have a large number of views, but new users might not be thinking too much about it. But you do need to think about it … it is one of the most important parts of your video. The reason is that when people are searching, they are going to be glancing at thumbnail images that the site displays in searches like this:

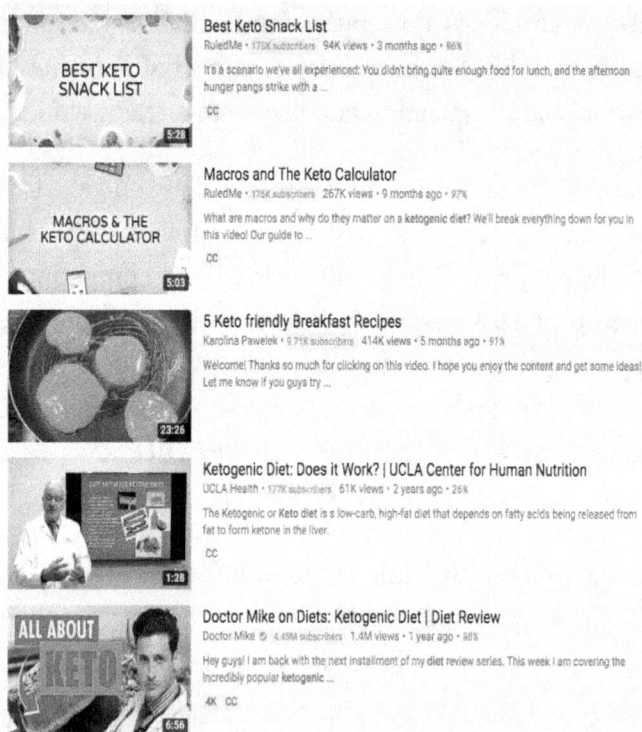

In this search, we used the phrase "keto diet." Notice the top two videos, they have the title of the video in the center of the image, against a background that makes the title stand out. This is a great way to draw attention to the video and to get people who are searching on the relevant topic to go ahead and click on it.

At the bottom, we also see a common method that is used. The person that uploaded that video has put a picture of themselves, along with the word KETO against a yellow background to make it really stand out. As you notice, it has 1.4 million views. The video just above it is from UCLA medical center, but it only has 61,000 views. There are many factors at play, of course, but the thumbnail is one thing that is going to help draw views because the video at the bottom simply stands out more, and it makes it clear that the video is about the topic that we searched for.

The video above the UCLA video has a horrible thumbnail – but the title of the video is an excellent title. The title is specific, and it is a phrase that people probably search for directly. While that video has had quite a bit of success, probably due to the very relevant title (and the owner of the channel may have a large number of subscribers), we believe it could have even more success if it had added some clear text like the bottom video in the image.

Here are some more examples of thumbnails. In this case, we searched for "make $100 a day".

Notice that these videos have clear text and imagery that will draw someone who is looking for information about making money. The first image at the top is probably the best because the solid orange background and readable text immediately makes it clear what the video is about. You don't even have to read the title of the video, because he has the title in the image. The last two images are also good too. These are examples that are not using the title, but rather the visual imagery of a $100 bill – together with a phrase that is pack with meaning. By saying copy and paste, they are telling you that in the video, they are going to show you the exact steps you need in order to make $100 a day.

Setting Up Your Video

Besides the thumbnail, you are going to want to think about keywords when making your video. Let's look at the last video in our second list of thumbnails. First, we can use Vid IQ to pull up the keywords that he used for the video.

This guy really knows what he is doing, notice that he ranks for almost every keyword. In fact, the video had more than 19,000 views after only being posted for two days.

Notice that he is using many long-tail keywords. If you are not familiar with long-tail keywords or using Google Keyword Planner, these are topics that you should become familiar with before getting your YouTube channel started. Remember that YouTube shows up in Google searches, and so you are going to want to choose keywords that people are searching for so that you can leverage the power of the YouTube site to show up in regular search engine results.

His title is also very good.

Make $100 Per Day For FREE To COPY and PASTE! (Earn Money Online)

The thing to notice about the title is that he has the main phrase that he is targeting, which is "Make $100 Per Day". Second, he used the word FREE, which is something that is going to pull people in, because a lot of people are always searching for free advice. This is followed by the phrase used in his thumbnail, COPY, and PASTE, which tells the viewer that he is going to show them the exact method they need to use in order to make $100 a day (we leave it for the reader to decide whether or not his method is valid). Finally, he has used another relevant key phrase in the title, which is "Earn Money Online."

Now let's look at his description. The first thing that

we want to examine is how the description is setup. Notice that he has put links both at the top and at the bottom of the description. A lot of YouTubers put their links at the bottom of the description, but this is a mistake, because many people who view the video aren't even going to open the description, much less scroll all the way to the bottom even if they do.

> Let's make money online! This method can make you $100 a day!
> My Top 2 Methods...
> Full eCom Training + Mentorship ⇐ https://ecomelites.com
> Full Affiliate Training + Mentorship ⇐ https://savageaffiliates.com
>
> Message me here for template: https://franklin.live/FreeNow
>
> Subscribe to Frank! https://franklin.live/Subscribe
> Follow Frank! https://franklin.live/Instagram
> Best Online Deals! https://franklin.live/BestDeals
>
> This is an awesome to way get started online for beginners! Its literally copy and paste and the best way to make money online in 2019.
>
> The first step is to go to a website called CB Engine. On this website you can from products that you can promote and earn online with. This is called affiliate marketing and its a great way to start online.
>
> Then you want to go to clickbank.com and sign up s you can get your affiliate link. You can use these links to make good money online. Make sure you promote products that are hot in the industry.
>
> When you want to make money online it's important to watch these tutorial videos all the way through. The next thing I do after signing up to Clickbank is I then go and find blogs online. Once I find the blogs I leave a comment in the comment section and leave my affiliate link in there. When someone clicks the like I will be paid just by working at home!
>
> This is a great way to work from home is to start doing affiliate marketing. Making money using this method is the best for beginners! You can do it for free, don't need a website and can do it from anywhere in the world!
>
> The best way to make money online and passive income from the internet is by watching this video all that way to the end. I give away some free content to help you scale this to the next level!
>
> ACCESS YOUR FREE TRAINING VIDEOS!
> FREE Ecom Training! https://franklin.live/Ecom
> FREE Affiliate Training! https://franklin.live/Affiliate

Now notice the text in the description. He is focusing on the keyword "Make Money Online," which is also used in his tags. Google will index the YouTube video, so put your main keyword in the description that goes with the video at least three times, but no more than five times. He also throws in 2019 in several places, so that he can simultaneously target Make Money Online 2019.

Another key phrase he has included in the description text is affiliate marketing. That also appears twice in the text. The word ClickBank is also present, which is a website for affiliate marketers, and so people searching for affiliate marketing may also be searching for ClickBank.

Promoting Your Video on Other Sites

After you have uploaded your video, you want to make some effort at organic promotion. The first way to do this is to post it on your Facebook page. When you do that, put a link in the description that takes people back to the YouTube page. Next, you will want to post it on Twitter. Also, create a blog post that goes with the video. If you write a transcript for your video, then put this text in the blog post with the video at the top of the page. Having the text in there will help get your blog post indexed by the search engines. You can also promote your video on other social media platforms and using it in answers you put up on Quora and in online forums.

Earning Money from YouTube

YouTube allows people to earn money with ads on their video channels. You have to become eligible for it and request it, but this is pretty easy. By adding advertisements to your videos, you can earn some extra money. And if you grow to the point where you are able to get millions of views, you can actually earn substantial money just from the advertisements on your YouTube videos alone.

Chapter 8:

Advertising on Facebook and YouTube

Now that we have learned how to set up a Facebook page and post videos on YouTube, it's time to talk about advertising. The fact is advertising with Facebook and YouTube is one of the best ways to do paid advertising that there has ever been. It is a very low-cost relative to other paid advertising methods, and it is also easy to set up and effective. There are a lot of people around who are going to give you negative spin about doing paid advertising, but quite frankly, we can't see doing without it in today's environment.

Facebook Advertising

The great power that comes with advertising on these sites is in the number of people you can reach for low-cost advertising, and the level of direct control and targeting that is available. We will start with Facebook advertising, which also covers Instagram advertising. The two are actually launched in the same campaigns by default, although you can choose to keep them distinct if that is your preference.

Audience Insights

The first thing to do when you are preparing to do Facebook advertising is to do some studying when it comes to the audience. Facebook gives you all the tools that you need in order to do this. You need to open up the Facebook advertising manager and go to the Audience Insights page.

The Facebook Audience Insights page lets you investigate audiences to see how large they are, look at their demographics, including gender, age, location, job title, and so forth, and most importantly, filter down by page likes. You will see that the page has an INTERESTS tab; this is where you want to focus in order to drill down your audience to find people who are interested in your niche.

One of the methods we use is that we find large competitors in our niche that are likely to have Facebook pages. This will enable us to target people that are already interested in the niche. It doesn't bother us that they have already bought from a competitor. Did the existence of McDonalds stop Burger King and Wendy's? In fact, it did the opposite – it encouraged them. So rather than fearing our competition, we choose to take advantage of players in our market.

So, when Facebook is asking you for interests when creating an audience, you can start by putting in the names of products or companies that are in the same niche. If you are selling organic food, then you are going to want to target people on Facebook who have liked the Whole Foods Facebook page. They are already interested in organic food (more than likely) and so they are probably going to be interested in your advertisement.

You can also target people by general interest, as well. So, in addition to targeting people that have liked Whole Foods, we could search for people that have liked organic foods and possibly people that have liked pages related to health.

You want to make your audience as specific as possible. When you make a more narrow focus, then you are more likely to get a large number of click-throughs.

As you narrow your audience down by page likes and interests, you are going to see your demographics change. Pay close attention to this and note it down. Be sure to save your audience. When you actually create your advertisements, you are going to be able to use the audience by clicking on Saved Audience.

Ad Type and Goal

When you create an advertisement, there are many different advertisement goals you can pursue. We will discuss two of them that are relevant to the kinds of businesses that we are discussing in this book. The first type of advertisement you can run is a page likes campaign. When you do this, you are going to associate your Facebook page with the ad. The purpose of the ad is specifically to drive Facebook users to your page. When they like it, this is similar to "friending" someone on Facebook. From then on, unless they unlike the page, every time you put up a post, it's going to show up on their own Facebook feed. Their friends and family will see it if they go to that person's Facebook feed, so this is a great way to expand your audience.

In the beginning, when you have just started a Facebook page, a likes campaign for a few days is a good idea. That way, you can get the page off the ground by getting an audience built.

The second type of ad that you are going to want to run on Facebook is a traffic campaign. The goal of a traffic campaign is to drive external traffic from Facebook to your website. If you have a storefront like a Shopify store, you can send them directly there. If you have an email landing page, then you can use that as the destination link.

Do not try to use affiliate marketing links in Facebook ads. They don't permit it, and doing so can actually get your ad account suspended or terminated. If you are selling affiliate products, we recommend that you create an email landing page that offers a free video or report if people sign up for your "newsletter," and then you can promote the affiliate offer from your emails after they have signed up. The landing page shouldn't give any indication that you are selling affiliate products, but it should definitely convey the niche that the affiliate product is involved in. Facebook allows ads that target email signup landing pages.

Budget

Facebook will suggest a budget of something on the order of $40 a day. But don't start off with that amount. In fact, you might not ever need it. One of the great things about Facebook advertising is that you can reach a significant level of customers on small budgets. So, start off with a budget of between $2-$5 per day. That sounds crazy, but it usually works.

After the ad has started running, you can gradually increase the budget until you get a level of traffic that you want to sustain. Remember that Facebook has 2.5 billion users, so the chances of you running out of customers in short order is next to nothing. You aren't going to reach more than a hundred or a couple hundred people per day if you are spending $5, but that is going to be enough to start driving significant numbers of email signups and possibly a couple of sales a day if your sales funnel is in good shape. If you find that it's working, then slowly increase the budget. Don't increase it more than fifty cents per day. You can also set up some variations of the ad so that you can do A/B testing. This can include different Facebook ads and also different landing pages. Then after 3-5 days, you simply kill what isn't working and then start increasing the budgets for those advertisements that do work.

When you are testing, you are going to want to look for failure at different points in the lifecycle. So, are you getting a lot of people clicking through, but they aren't signing up for the email? Maybe the copy or images on your landing page are not very good. Alternatively, are they not clicking through to the website? Then maybe the text or media used in your ad are not very good. Take a look at these things and make adjustments as necessary.

Media

Facebook allows you to create a few different types of ads. The default type of ad is a single image, and believe it or not; this still works very well. You can also run video ads, which work very well also. There is also the possibility of making an on the fly video ad from still images using their technology, which will add text and some interesting effects to the manufactured video. We haven't tried this one yet, but it looks like it could be very effective. They also have slide show ads, which can show multiple images or a carousel that can mix images and videos.

In our view, simple is best. We are really not impressed with the idea of making someone go through multiple videos and images unless you are trying to push multiple products in one ad, like showing them that you sell many different t-shirts on your website. Single image ads work very well for driving traffic if the image is relevant and done well. Video ads, of course, do work extremely well.

You can use your own images, but Facebook also makes stock images from Shutterstock available for use without charge.

Platform Options

You can advertise on Facebook feeds, in messaging, in stories, on the right-hand side, and on Instagram. The default option is to advertise everywhere, and we recommend that *you* start with this and then kill any options that are not producing. For some of the ads that we have run, for example, we got many clicks for ads that were shown in the Facebook feed, but very few on Instagram and so we cut Instagram. Facebook provides very comprehensive reporting, and so you will be able to get a clear picture of what is working and what isn't working.

YouTube Advertising

YouTube advertising is another low-cost way to reach a large number of people. With YouTube advertising, you don't even have to create anything special for an ad if you don't want to, provided that you have videos on your channel ready to use.

YouTube advertising, surprisingly enough, is about video. So, you are going to make a video that you want to use in an advertisement and then upload it to your channel, or if you have a video already up there that you think is suitable, then you can use that instead. For videos that you want to advertise with, shorter is better. A 30 second to one-minute video is ideal for making an advertisement.

An advertisement can be sophisticated or not. People on YouTube are not going to be put off by a regular video that they are used to seeing on the site anyway. The point is to put up a good video that people are going to find compelling enough to watch.

In your video, one thing that you want to do is include a call to action. So, this is either going to be you telling them to click to go to your website or putting up a screen in the video with text that tells them where to go.

Leveraging Videos

The fun starts after you have uploaded the video that you are planning to use in your ad. You are going to be taken to a web page where you can specify the usual information, such as daily budget, keywords to target, and so forth. One of the most interesting features of the advertising interface is that you can pick specific videos where your ad is going to run. So, you can pick videos that have large numbers of views, so that you can be assured of having a large audience for your advertisement. When doing this, be sure to do some research ahead of time. You want to find out when videos were uploaded and whether or not they are getting current views or if they racked up a lot of views in the past. If a video has 2 million views, but it got that five years ago, then it is not going to be useful for this purpose. A video that has only been up a week and has 100,000 views is probably going to be more useful.

You can select multiple videos to use. You don't want

to use too many but select between 3-10 videos.

Budget

A good thing about advertising on YouTube is that it's a low budget activity. So, you can reach a lot of people for pennies on the dollar. In our testing, we have set budgets of $5 a day and gotten thousands of views. We don't know how it's going to work out in your case, but you should be able to advertise on YouTube without having to spend huge amounts of money.

Chapter 9:

Passive Income

If you are reading this book, then you are definitely convinced of the value of using social media to get followers. However, what is the end goal? The end goal for many is to set up a largely passive income stream. Of course, nothing is going to be entirely passive, but you can get a passive income stream in the sense that you are only going to have to work an hour or two a day at the most once you get everything set up and running.

Work Now, Payoff Later

The most important part of a passive income stream is to put in work now that is going to pay off in the future. If you are putting quality content, whether it is on your blog, your YouTube channel, Instagram, or your Facebook page, it is going to be out there on the internet, getting traffic for months and years to come. As long as all of your links are working, and your users are being directed to working landing pages and sales pages, this means that months and years after you have set these pages up and put posts on social media, they are going to be generating sales and income for you.

As time goes on, if you are continually adding content, and therefore getting viewed by search engines like Google as an authority, you are going to be driving more and more organic traffic. You will probably always want to include advertising as a part of your approach, but you are going to find that as time goes on, you are getting higher levels of organic income.

One of the mistakes that a lot of people make is that they think they are going to get organic traffic right away, but then it doesn't happen, and so they think the business is a failure. This is a huge mistake because organic traffic is something that builds up slowly – but surely – over an extended time period providing that you keep adding to your content. The key to success is quality content that has a lot of value.

In most cases, organic traffic works in exponential fashion. An exponential curve starts off with a very slow rise, and then it suddenly accelerates to high values. This is how organic web traffic often works. In the first weeks and months of your efforts, it's going to seem like you are getting nowhere because you are only going to have a trickle of traffic. But if you are persistent and stick with it, months down the road, you are going to start seeing your traffic increase rapidly.

Consistency Is the Key

Setting up both a daily and weekly routine to post for your business is going to be an important part of getting a passive income to work. Continually posting content is a large part of the secret to success. So, you want to have a routine where you always follow the same steps so that nothing gets neglected. The specific ways that you post are not as important as setting up a posting routine and then carrying it out. Here is a sample routine:

- Post to Facebook : 3 times a week, on Tuesday, Thursday, and Saturday.

- Post to Twitter: At least once per day.

- Post to Instagram: Twice per day.

- Post to Pinterest: Monday and Friday.

- Post to blog: Sunday, Tuesday, and Thursday. Post blog posts on Facebook and Twitter.

- Post video to YouTube: Once a week, every Thursday.

The specifics in this plan can work for some people, but they really don't matter, come up with your own schedule if you like. Some may not use Pinterest, and in its place, you can post another video to YouTube. The value of regular posting, however, can't be said enough. This has two benefits. The first is getting you into a disciplined habit of continually adding content. This is the most important factor for growing passive income that is going to come from organic traffic. The second factor is adding some anticipation for your followers on social media.

Using YouTube as an example, as you get better at making videos and get channel subscribers, people are going to start anticipating your videos if they are passionate about your niche. As you build a following, and you start dropping videos every Monday and Thursday, say, your following is going to eagerly anticipate the arrival of your videos. That is going to help drive views. If you are using advertising to monetize your channel, that is going to help you earn more money, and you will also be getting regular visits to your main website and other social media sites.

If your content is compelling, then your subscribers are going to be sharing it with their friends, helping you to grow even more and get extra free traffic.

Free and Paid Traffic Leads to Passive Income

For passive income, that doesn't mean you never work

at all. It means that you are not working a 40-hour workweek or even 20 hours. It doesn't take long to set up a Facebook ad, and after that, all you have to do is occasionally check it to keep tabs on things and make occasional adjustments. In the meantime, every day, the ads are going to be driving hundreds of people to your websites, and some people are going to be buying your products. After the ad is established, then you are only going to have to spend 10 or 20 minutes checking out results, and it might be generating $100-$300 a day in income for you.

Finding Offers to Sell

Running a passive income business is something that is more suitable for electronic products. These are products that are sold and consumed online, so they are information products. They can be how-to guides, training courses, or software. Once they are made, you don't have to worry about maintaining them. It is also possible to set up a drop shipping business, but that is a bit more work.

Let's talk about information products first, and about the idea of creating your own information products. Keep in mind that you don't have to create your own information products. As we will see in a minute, there are plenty of places to find products that you can sell as an affiliate, and you can actually make really good money doing so. But there are some drawbacks to being an affiliate, which is something that we are also going to discuss.

The first thing to think about is whether or not you know enough about a subject to make an information product. In most cases, the answer is yes. The reason is that you only have to know a little bit more than the general public knows. You can start with things that you are passionate about now. Is there any way that you could turn that passion into teaching about it? Again, you don't have to be a doctor to do it.

There are two ways that you can go about it. The first and easiest way is to create a book in PDF format. Then you can sell the book online. Depending on how extensive the book is, you can charge anywhere from $17-$27. Many people are going to say, "what about Kindle"? That is a valid question, but the truth is if you write a book and then publish it on major bookstores, you are going to make pennies. To make a living that way, you have to publish a large number of books. They only sell for $2.99, and most books are free to read, but you get paid by the online store, fractions of a penny per page. This isn't to say that the model can't work, but unless you want to write and publish a huge number of books, that is not going to be something that many people are going to be interested in pursuing. With the online model, you can be making up to $47 per sale.

The second option is more lucrative and provides more value to the customer, and therefore you can charge more money. This method is to create a video course. Depending on the subject and how much value your course provides, you can charge anywhere from $47 all the way up to $1,000 or more. You can host your course on a website called Kajabi, that offers a full-blown suite of tools for businesses that are selling video education courses. They manage everything for you, including having a comment system, ways to drip release your video course, quizzes, and a setup for people to contact you for support. They also have a login system that will assign your users' login names and passwords, and they manage the security. This isn't an advertisement for Kajabi, and we are just letting readers know that there are full-blown sites available so that you don't have to reinvent the wheel, as far as having a secured video course website.

Affiliate Marketing

Now let's talk about affiliate marketing. For many readers, the idea of creating your own video course sounds intimidating, and it might not even be something that you want to do. The good news is that there are many affiliate marketing courses that can be used to sell physical and digital goods online. JVZoo and ClickBank are two that are worth checking out. You can find affiliate products in nearly every niche on these sites, and many that pay out high commissions.

When you visit ClickBank, as an example, you can go to their marketplace. You can either browse by category or search by specific keywords. On ClickBank, they also provide a useful metric called gravity. This tells you how many affiliates sold at least one copy of a product over the past 12 weeks. The rule of thumb is that any product that has a gravity of 20 and above is worth promoting. There are some very strong products that have gravity scores over 200, but one of the downsides of high gravity products is that this also means that a ton of people are on the internet promoting the product. If you are late to the game, the buying public might be saturated, having seen the product offered to them by a bunch of people many times. A high gravity product has also probably been advertised on Facebook many times.

There are other ways to sell affiliate products, as well. Many services like Bluehost web hosting will pay you an affiliate commission if you get someone to sign up for their service. You can also sell Amazon products as an affiliate, but the commissions in these cases are going to be a lot lower than what you get selling something like a ClickBank product, where you can earn $20 up to hundreds of dollars per sale.

So, let's talk about the advantages of affiliate products. The first advantage is a big one – it saves you the hassle of creating your own product from scratch. The second advantage is you can find products that are already market-tested. Typically, a ClickBank product owner has put a large amount of effort into building out their website and researching the niche so that they know it is something that can get large numbers of sales. Another advantage is often ClickBank sellers will provide you with many selling tools that you can use. So, you can use their emails that are proven to convert, and they may have many product images, banners, logos, and other materials that you can use to promote the product.

There are some downsides to ClickBank products as well. One of them is that affiliate marketing links are frowned upon by many websites. This includes Facebook, unfortunately, and if you try to run an ad on Facebook that goes directly to an affiliate marketing link, you are likely to have the ad pulled (if it is approved at all) and you might even get your account suspended or terminated, depending on what kind of affiliate offer you were promoting. One thing to watch out for is internet marketing training courses. In other words, there are a lot of people out there who sell courses that teach people how to set up and run an

Internet business. To get an idea of what we are talking about, go on Google and look up "John Cristani." Now is John Cristani legitimate? We believe he is completely legitimate. The problem is not him, but Facebook simply doesn't allow you to advertise for the type of training that he provides. They have labeled it a "get rich quick" scheme, and they are very strict about it.

That means that if you are selling an affiliate product, you are going to have to put some work in to create your own website. Hopefully, you have one already, but all you need for the purposes of selling an affiliate product is a landing page.

Another downside to selling affiliate products is that you are going to be competing with a significant number of other people selling the same product. That means that you are going to have a harder time breaking through to get sales of your own. When you are posting videos about it on YouTube, there might be ten or twenty other people doing the same thing.

One thing that can work in your favor, however, is most affiliate marketers are not very good (although there are definitely some real pros out there). This is something that you can observe on YouTube on a regular basis. When a new product is released, you will see the amateurs simply post a video on YouTube that they stole or borrowed (or even used with permission) from the owner of the product, and they don't offer any real value of their own. One thing that we can advise is that if you are selling affiliate marketing products, you can give yourself a real edge if you offer some value of your own.

This can be done in many different ways. For starters, instead of just slapping yet another copy of the same video on YouTube, make your own video that offers some value that is directly related to the niche. If you are serious about marketing the product, get the product and offer a real, genuine review of it. In many cases, the seller on ClickBank will give you a review copy, but those are harder to get than they used to be because many affiliates abused the privilege and posted them for download online. But if you are attempting to make a serious effort at starting a business that is built around the product, then buying it so that you can genuinely review it is probably a worthwhile investment.

There are several ways you can publish reviews. Publish one on your blog, provided that you have a blog that is directly related to the niche. You can also post your reviews on social media sites. This step would suppose that you have a good, usually non-salesy relationship with your followers. This is where the trust that you build up over time with your social media followers can come into play. If you are a trusted voice in the niche, and you are providing good content to your social media followers that has a lot of actionable value on a regular basis, it will be OK to periodically recommend an affiliate product. And since they trust you, many of your followers are probably going to end up buying the product. But don't abuse your position. If you push a bad product, that will destroy the trust that you have spent so much time building up with your users. If you put up a lot of spammy posts that simply try to sell an affiliate product, that is going to turn off a lot of your followers, and many of them will drop out and unfollow you, unfriend you, and unsubscribe. So, when it comes to pushing affiliate marketing products on social media sites, remember that less is often more.

Another way to promote affiliate marketing products that works quite well is to put up a website that reviews related products. Then post a long, thorough, and genuine review of the product. You can incorporate a video from YouTube in the review, but be sure to target the right keywords and include a lot of text. These days, Google is also giving points for having a few images on your web page, as well. They recognize that people are attracted by visual content, so sometimes a web page that has a couple of images placed among the text is going to do better than one that is just text alone.

So how much can you make as an affiliate marketer? The cold hard truth is most people make little to no money. But the reason that they don't make any money is that they fail to put the effort required, or they make bad decisions like posting the same exact video 30 others posted. If you take it seriously and learn the skills necessary to build a business with it, you can make anywhere from $50,000 up to $1 million a year.

Chapter 10:

Sales Methods

In this chapter, we are going to talk about closing a sale, with techniques that are going to be useful whether or not you have your own product or are pushing an affiliate marketing product. Something that is interesting is these techniques were developed many years ago, but they still work very well.

When the Internet first got started, it was possible to run a pay per click ad on Google or Yahoo and include an affiliate link directly in the ad, and so you could get easy sales just pushing traffic to a sales page for a product. For some reason, the powers that be in Google decided that this was unacceptable behavior. So, they began to ban direct linking via affiliate links. We have seen similar behavior by others, such as Facebook.

Marketers needed to come up with a new strategy, and by 2008 people were using email marketing to great effect. This was used before that, of course, but it was around that time that it became the standard go-to marketing method. Today, it is as widespread as ever, and almost every website that you visit is going to have some kind of email signup form.

Email Marketing

So, what is email marketing? Email marketing uses emails combined with affiliate links (or links to your own product pages) that push traffic in the hopes of making sales. It has a high conversion rate, because people have to voluntarily sign up to join your email list. If you are honest about what the purpose of the email list is, then you are likely to be able to drive sales from it. So, what do we mean when we say being honest? That means that you are using your email list for the same niche that you told people about in the first place. Each email list that you create should be for one specific niche and not discuss unrelated topics.

An email marketing scheme will send people multiple emails after they sign up for your newsletter or whatever you want to call it. Typically, you will send out emails every day for a few days, and then start tapering off the frequency. If you want to build up a large list and keep it going for a long time, you might want to periodically email them about important news or tips related to the niche topic.

In your emails, you don't always want to do a hard sell. The first email should be a long email that has a lot of discussion about the niche topic. Then at the end of the email, you can recommend the product you are selling with a link. You should continue this approach for a couple of emails after that, and then you can send out an email with a hard sell. The truth is, after this point, if people have not purchased, most of them are not going to, but sometimes you do get some late adopters.

To have an email marketing system, you are not going to manually send out the emails, that would be far too much work. The way you want to do it is using an autoresponder service. They will collect the email addresses for you from customers and send out your emails at regular intervals each time a customer signs up. Some of the good autoresponder services that are available include Get Response, AWeber, and Mail Chimp.

Sales Funnel

An email marketing campaign is something that is a part of what is called a sales funnel. A sales funnel is just a small number of websites that are used to close a sale. The first page that people are going to encounter in the funnel is a signup form where you offer them a free gift in exchange for signing up for your email list. The free gift can be a short book or a video mini-course. The point is to offer them some real value in order to get them to sign up for your email list.

When they sign up, they will be directed to the second web page that is in the funnel. There are different ways you can set this up, and some people actually send the customer directly to the sales page of the product after they sign up for the newsletter. Alternatively, you can have them go to a second page that does a little "preselling" of the product. For example, you could have your review of an affiliate product posted here. The page will have buttons or links on it to take them to the sales page if they are interested.

If they are not interested, it's not a big deal because now you have their email address, and you can email them at any time. So, you can email them and use more gentle persuasion to buy the product or to sell other products to them. The same general principle applies, don't be too salesy in your approach. If people are getting a lot of hard sell emails in their inbox, then they will either stop reading your emails or, worse, unsubscribe from the list altogether.

The sales funnel can also be used to push more offers, called upsells. So, you can have additional steps in the funnel. You can try and sell people more expensive products in the same niche using the other pages in the funnel, or "downsell" them by offering them a book or something that is cheaper. These methods have been tested over and over again, and if you set it up right, they work. Of course, doing it right means having a nice-looking website and the right sales copy. If you are not sure about this or don't have much experience, try looking at what other people are doing to get some examples of how to set things up.

There are many services that you can use to set up a sales funnel using drag and drop functionality. There is no reason to try and build a website from scratch when everything is already made for you. One service to strongly consider is called Get Response. The reason that a lot of marketers like Get Response is that it incorporates the ability to build a sales funnel with an email autoresponder.

One of the best services for building a sales funnel is called ClickFunnels. This site was designed by expert internet marketers who made their first million on ClickBank as affiliates. So, they know exactly what is needed to build a sales funnel, and they provide it for you. It comes with a large number of drag and drop templates that make it easy, and you can incorporate the pages you create into a blog or website, or you can have them hosted there and even register new domain names. You can set up email autoresponders in the service, but it is better, in our opinion, to use an external email autoresponder like AWeber or Mail Chimp, and this can be integrated into your ClickFunnels projects quite easily.

Driving Traffic

Of course, a sales funnel isn't any good without traffic. We have actually talked a great deal about driving traffic already, that is what your social media presence is ultimately for. You can have your sales funnel as the link on your Instagram profile, you can link to it every time that you post a YouTube video, and you can link to it from your blog and from Facebook.

Paid traffic can also be used in conjunction with a sales funnel. Of course, you can use Facebook ad campaigns to drive traffic to a sales funnel. You can also use old-time pay-per-click advertising. Google and Yahoo/Bing can both be used. Bing doesn't appeal as much to people, but Bing will drive a large amount of traffic to our sites. The traffic on Bing is generally quite a bit cheaper than you have to spend to advertise on Google.

There are also some other options that can be used for paid advertising, but many of them are of dubious value. One possibility that is frequently discussed is "network" advertising. These are ads that you see on many websites that are often square-shaped with an image and some text below. They are found on many major websites, but the problem with this type of advertising is that it is not well-targeted. As a hypothetical example, suppose that you are running these types of ads, but they are being displayed on generic websites like CNN, say. In that case, the overall audience is very large, but the downside is that very few people in that audience are going to be interested in your niche. Generally, a niche is going to apply to a small subset of the overall population, but most people are not going to be very interested. So, your ad is going to be showing for no real purpose. If you are paying for impressions, then you are going to go bankrupt very fast because you could get a lot of impressions on those big websites without getting any clicks or sales.

What you want is targeted advertising. Search engine advertising works because people are searching for related keywords that you specify when you create the ad. So those people are already interested in the topic to begin with, and many of those people are actually on the search engines because they are interested in buying a product that is going to help them solve a problem that is related to that niche.

On Facebook or Instagram, you can target people who have demonstrated in the past that they are interested in a particular niche, by liking Facebook pages that are related to your niche in some way. So, if you are going to use paid traffic, our suggestion is to use Google PPC, YouTube, Bing, and Facebook. Between these networks (which also covers Instagram), you have covered literally everyone in the general public.

You can also, when appropriate, directly advertise on other social media sites like Pinterest. Before you do so, be sure that people that are using the site that you pick are interested in your product or service in some way. Remember that on Pinterest, the audience is largely female, and so if you are selling something that men only are interested in, then you are not going to have very much success with your advertising efforts on that site.

There are other tricks that you can try to use for promotion. One that has been suggested by some internet marketers is a social media contest. You can run a Facebook contest, or an Instagram giveaway to try and generate some hype among your followers. When you are doing this, hopefully, your current followers will share the information and bring in some new prospects that will become followers and possibly visit your sales funnel and sign up for the email list.

There are some older tricks that people have also used to varying degrees of success. One method that has worked for *some* people is posting craigslist ads for affiliate marketing products they are selling. This may or may not work depending on luck. The good thing about this approach is that it is free, and Craigslist gets a huge amount of traffic. The bad thing about this is the site is policed by independent zealots that will flag your post as inappropriate. If that happens, the ad will be taken down, but you could even get "banned" from the site, although you might be able to sneak back on using a different email address.

We haven't tried this method, but we have known people that got a lot of sales doing it. A different approach may be to try it without using a direct affiliate link. That might not offend the hardcore people that are on Craigslist as much as an affiliate link would. But again, keep in mind that we haven't tried it, so try at your own risk!

Summary

An email list is a central part of closing the sale, once you have driven traffic to your website. The gateway to your website is going to be a sales funnel. The sales funnel takes the customer through several steps to encourage them to purchase products. Social media and paid advertising are the best ways to get traffic to your sales funnel so that you can get customers to sign up and buy your products and services. You can also try other "guerilla marketing" methods.

Conclusion

Thank you for making it through to the end of Influencer Marketing, let's hope it was informative and able to provide you with all of the tools you need to achieve your goals whatever they may be.

If you have made it all the way through the book, you will have a more thorough understanding of social media, what sites are the most important, and how to utilize them in order to drive traffic to your business and build a solid following.

Reading a book is only the first step. Now that you have some idea of what to do, you should get started building your business. One of the unfortunate things about our era is that despite the wealth of information that is available, and all of the tools that can be exploited to reach customers, is the fact that only a small fraction of people that take courses, read books, or follow videos on starting a new business online ever take action. Simply taking action is an important step on the road to success. If you don't try, of course, you are not going to fail, and you can keep doing what you are doing now. But among those who take the appropriate steps, many are going to reach a new level of success.

We sincerely hope that we have provided our readers

with a significant amount of actionable information. It isn't necessary to get on every social media website or app, and in fact, it's better to establish a solid presence on a few key sites.

In our view, the next steps are to start by preparing yourself properly to deal with a flow of customers first. That means setting up your sales funnel, having a clear sales message and lead magnet, and then having a systematic way to connect your social media posting and advertising to the sales funnel.

Once you have that step-down, you can use paid advertising to start driving traffic immediately. Once you launch paid advertising on social media, you are going to find that it is nearly instant. You can use this to your advantage if things are not working out right away, and if you find that you don't get instant success, don't get discouraged. If things are not working out, take a close look at your sales funnel, and make adjustments. You might have to make changes to the colors or images used on your site, or perhaps change your sales copy. Test, test, and test again is one bit of advice that you should remember when it comes to marketing.

If you are looking to improve your education, there are many resources that are available online. You can find many of these resources free of charge. On YouTube, there are many expert marketers who make free videos that can help you learn how to make an income online. You can also find people that will teach you how to use social media websites and apps in order to build your own following, and then how to leverage it to drive traffic to your own sales funnel, where you can turn eyeballs into paying customers.

Finally, you can also utilize the educational site Udemy, where many experts offer their advice in reasonably priced courses. But most of all, besides educating yourself, be sure to take action! Best of luck to all of our readers!

Finally, if you found this book useful in any way, a review on Amazon is always appreciated!

www.ingramcontent.com/pod-product-compliance
Lightning Source LLC
Chambersburg PA
CBHW072030230526
45466CB00020B/1208